BEHAVING BRAVELY
HOW TO MINDSHIFT LIFE'S CHALLENGES

BEHAVING BRAVELY
HOW TO MINDSHIFT LIFE'S CHALLENGES

BY
ANITA K
WITH MICHAEL ASHLEY

Behaving Bravely

Copyright © 2019 by Anita K

ISBN: 9781077291164

Contents

Behaving Bravely

This Book is...

~Inspired by my father, Kanti~
"I commit to carry out a bigger purpose beyond myself for others around me."

~Dedicated to my daughter, Sanam~
"Know when you commit to something beyond yourself, a true achievement will follow."

In experiencing you both, I have humbly learned the meaning of commitment.

Foreword

Watching contemporary American movies and TV, you might think every South Asian is either a doctor, a computer whiz, or some other kind of academic overachiever. Like all ethnic stereotypes, this is an overly broad and unfair characterization—but one containing a kernel of truth.

In the South Asian culture, parents expect much from their offspring: to be a "golden child," a straight-A student who goes on to become a successful doctor, lawyer, or millionaire entrepreneur. The drive to distinguish yourself academically, professionally, and financially is baked in from birth. Of course, not all South Asians are destined for a "safe" career. Some of us desire other things. We want to be chefs, coaches, artists, innovators, athletes.

And, in my case, an actor.

As a kid, I was far more interested in music and films than other South Asians of my age. None of my friends had much enthusiasm for acting or filmmaking. Luckily, my brother shared my artistic proclivities, and together we would film skits and mini-movies. I was equally lucky that while members of the South Asian community can be a bit judgmental and gossipy, my parents fully supported me when I announced I wanted to become a professional actor.

Of course, they were concerned about show business's reputation for unpredictability and my limited chances of making a living as a performer, regardless of how much talent or training I might possess. Other members of my extended family weren't so charitable. They discouraged me from what they saw as a foolish pursuit. In fact, just about everyone I knew saw my desire to act as a "phase" that I would eventually outgrow.

To keep peace in my family, I kept my interest in the arts compartmentalized as I continued to receive a "traditional" education in a profession promising a steady income upon graduation. However, when my first break occurred—I was offered a part in the 2011 made-for-TV high school fantasy/comedy *Teen Spirit*—I happily hopped off the academic track and committed myself full time to performing. I decided I didn't care what anyone else thought. I was going to do what made me happy.

This is what we call being one's "authentic self." It's the only path to true happiness I'm aware of. And it's the focus of Anita K's BRAVE program, of which I'm a huge and enthusiastic fan. Without a doubt, I understand why being brave, why finding the courage to pursue things that make you happy and fulfilled, can be difficult for many people.

Unfortunately, we are all scarred by childhood fears and traumas, by life's failures and disappointments. We also live in a time in which many of our most fundamental rights and cherished beliefs are under assault. Breaking free of social constraints takes daring and a willingness to endure judgment and criticism, often from those closest to us. Personally, I have nothing but respect for those who choose to venture beyond their comfort zones to seek a better career, better relationships, greater wisdom, or just a better life.

Anita herself is a great example of this at work. She wasn't fulfilled in either her marriage or professional life. Even though she did her best to hang on, sought professional counseling, and explored outside solutions, she realized she needed to create her own program if she was going to achieve any degree of personal happiness. Which is exactly what she did. In the process, she discovered that she loved helping others, thus turning a series of setbacks into a successful and meaningful life's calling. Through her brave example, she shows us that if you adhere to your principles and hold yourself accountable, victory—*and joy*—can be yours.

Fundamental to Anita's approach is a term she coined: *benevolief.* A combination of the words "benevolent" and "belief," the first part is critical, because most of us cling to beliefs that are, for lack of a better word, "malevolent." We may believe "we're not good enough." That we're "too young," "too old," "too inexperienced," or "over-qualified" for whatever it is we seek. Too often we believe the "odds are stacked against us;" that "the game is rigged."

All these beliefs do is hold us back.

Yet, Anita reminds us we can only achieve the things we believe we *can* achieve. Her timely message is that it's essential we approach any problem, situation, or challenge from the most positive angle. Anita also emphasizes the need to *mindbreak* to *mindshift*. Paradigm-changing, these two activities describe the incredible power of transforming yourself from the inside out to improve your world. For years, I've practiced similar techniques, including creating *vision boards*, to foster the type of thinking that will create desired life changes. Like Anita, I believe if you put out good thoughts and energy, this positivity will eventually become manifest.

Beyond these simple but profound concepts, BRAVE provides a structure for personal development. It's a roadmap for attaining your goals, whatever they may be. Likewise, each chapter's exercises force you to dig deeply, to reach the core of who you are as an individual. Along with helpful affirmations and illustrative case studies, the book's powerful material can shine a light on what's needed to make the changes you wish to see in your life.

Ultimately, I am so thrilled that Anita finally put her principles into print so others can benefit and grow. We all need to conquer our fears. We all need to find happiness. We all need to discover our authentic selves.

We all need to be BRAVE.

~Paras Patel, Los Angeles, June 2019

*****

Paras Patel is a professional actor. A first-generation Indian-American now living in Los Angeles, his credits include the TV series *The Chosen, Revolution, NCIS: Los Angeles, Nashville, Ray Donovan,* and *Fresh Off the Boat,* as well as the movies: *Teen Spirit* and *The Duff.*

Chapter 1
Bravery Now

"Your strength, your beauty, your answers are in your journey; always keep going."

What, Another Self-Help Book?

Over the past 100 years, literally hundreds of books have been published offering people ways to find happiness and success. From Dale Carnegie's *How to Win Friends and Influence People* (1936), to motivational expert Tony Robbins' *Unlimited Power* (1987), to Rhonda Byrne's *The Secret* (2006), writers, psychologists, lecturers, and business gurus have offered readers directions on how to live longer, healthier, more fulfilling lives. How to get rich. How to find love. How to raise children. How to lose weight. How to live to be 100. How to find meaning in life. No aspect of the human condition has gone unaddressed.

Yet, we all seek answers. And it's no wonder why. Many of us feel troubled and confused. Society has developed innumerable ways to make us anxious. Advertisers tell us we're not beautiful enough, not exciting enough, not cool enough. We're too fat or too thin. Too young or too old. We don't wear the right clothes. We don't drive the right cars. We don't use the right technology or wear the right body spray. We don't have enough fun. If we would just buy this particular toothpaste, lease this car, line up for this smartphone, swallow this pill, take this cruise, or vote for this political candidate, then we'd make more money, have more friends, appear more attractive, be more productive, feel better, and just be so much happier.

But it's not just our culture or big business getting into our heads. Friends and family members can, knowingly or even unknowingly, use their relationships with us to undermine our self-confidence. Parents question our choices and decisions well into adulthood. Children challenge our fitness, taste, and judgment. Friends voice disapproval of our behavior or offer advice on everything from our fashion choices to our restaurant selections. They all just want to help us, of course. But, over time, the nit-picking and criticism can leave permanent scars.

The rise of social media hasn't made things any easier. Platforms like Facebook and Instagram promise to connect us, yet often end up amplifying the volume of critical messages. Does this sound familiar? You have friends who share photos of their latest luxury vacations, home remodeling projects, or royalty-scale weddings. Instead of making you feel connected to them, these glimpses into their lives leave you feeling less than.

Our tech age miracles bring other new vexing challenges. We're expected to be accessible on our phones day and night—on the weekends and even holidays. But so much screen time makes us nervous, leading to self-doubts. Meanwhile, cyberbullying has become an epidemic, particularly among school-age children who use social media to harass their peers. Perhaps it's no wonder the suicide rate for teens between 10 and 17 years jumped 70 percent between 2006 and 2016, according to the Centers for Disease Control and Prevention.

Access to so much information has come at a cost. Instead of embracing our reflections, too often we become our own worst critics. So many of us create idealized versions of ourselves we can never live up to. Even those people most of us would consider successful—celebrities, political leaders, champion athletes, captains of industry—are often plagued by the same insecurities. It turns out the so-called imposter syndrome—the feeling that you're "faking it" and aren't really as capable as others believe—is shockingly common among top executives and leading money-earners.

So how can one more self-help book help?

The Eternal Outsider

Like so many of you, I, too, spent years seeking a path to happiness. For part of my life I felt lost, depressed, unfulfilled. Even what success I enjoyed was always tempered with the gnawing feeling whatever I did was never quite good enough.

Part of this anxiety came from my background. I am an Indian-American woman born in the United States at a time when people of South Asian ancestry were far less common than they are today. Because of my name, skin color, and facial features, I spent much of my childhood feeling like an outsider. It didn't matter that, as a native-born American, I spoke perfect, unaccented American English, or that I shared the same cultural references, that I grew liking the same TV shows, movies, and music as my peers. I still couldn't help feeling exotic due to the way I looked and my background.

To be fair, no one used racial slurs to my face in school or openly discriminated against me, yet I couldn't help feeling apart from my classmates. In time, I accepted the outsider's role. I took it in stride that I would never really belong, and that the easy confidence and security afforded many of my white-skinned peers would forever be beyond my reach. As a child growing up in suburban Orange County, California, I didn't question or challenge this notion. Instead, I used it to form my mental and emotional matrix.

Add to this situation a sexual abuse incident I never reported nor spoke of openly—as well as feelings of inferiority from not living up to my parents' expectations—and you can get a sense of why I felt out of place for so long. Individually and in combination, these traumas left me feeling weak and unworthy. In purely scientific terms, I was what behavioral psychologists might call "confused."

One of the deepest desires I can recall feeling as a child was a longing to change. I desired to be one of those successful, carefree women I saw on television. I also wanted to look like all of the other girls in my class, with their straight blonde hair and white skin. More than this, I wished to measure up to my dad's expectations, to prove myself as smart as he seemed to effortlessly be. Most of all, I wanted to be happy.

But as much as I wanted to change, I was also *afraid* to change. Like a kidnap victim who comes to identify with her kidnapper, I developed a kind of emotional Stockholm syndrome. It's weird to say, but I actually came to embrace my misery. Fear became my identity. I became comfortable in the box I had put myself in. It wasn't until age 45 that life forced me to make a radical—and needed— transformation.

A New Career, a New Outlook

Before getting into what forced me to change, let me offer the broad strokes of my professional life. Since graduating college, I have spent most of my time working in the tech industry. Not as a programmer—at least I avoided *that* Indian stereotype—but in human resources. For reasons I cannot explain, I tended to become a kind of father confessor to my co-workers, someone in whom they could comfortably confide and seek advice. Perhaps I naturally radiated a sense of empathy that attracted people. Maybe I just had the ability to listen without judgment, a quality I've come to discover is rare. Or maybe people just saw me as non-threatening and a convenient place to unload whatever emotional burdens were weighing them down.

Whatever the reason, counseling became a side business for me. Something I became good at. Co-workers, family members, even some of my corporate clients began coming to me for advice and guidance, and the responses I provided were solid enough that they came back for more. But, speaking of faking it until you make it, the truth is, at the same time I was helping others, I was still dealing with my own feelings of inadequacy relating to a failed marriage. Try as I might, all of these burdens affected me financially, professionally, physically, emotionally, and yes, even spiritually. I felt like my life was still dangerously out of balance.

In the midst of so much upheaval—some good and some bad—I heard about life coaching. At first, the subject just piqued my curiosity, but little by little, I felt drawn to it like nothing before. Here was a profession in which being an outsider could actually be a good thing. At last, all of the challenges I had faced—all the many times I felt unseen and unheard—could be channeled for good. I could turn my fear and struggle into something positive for others.

After investigating coaching more, I decided to see whether or not this could be a viable second career. Even if I couldn't do it professionally, I believed working through the training curriculum would help me get my life on track and support my personal development. It turned out receiving life coach training was one of the best professional and personal decisions I ever made.

What is a Life Coach?

If you're not familiar with the term, you may be asking, "Just what *is* a life coach?" Although the concept has been around for a while, it does not have a specific, widely recognized definition. This can lead to misunderstandings. Life coaching is a practice in which a trusted adviser partners with clients to help them achieve their goals by identifying their personal situation and challenges, then offering solutions achievable through education, retraining, and reframing habits and behavioral patterns. Support needs to be individualized, customized, and practical.

The best life coaches wear many hats as they seek holistic, game-changing ways to tap into a client's full potential as a person. *Newsweek* defines the role this way: "Part consultant, part motivational speaker, part therapist, and part rent-a-friend, [life] coaches work with managers, entrepreneurs, and just about anyone, helping them define and achieve their goals—career, personal, or most often, both." No advanced degree is required to become a life coach, although professional training and certification is recommended.

So, what qualifications do I hold that allow me to do this professionally? In addition to my bachelor's degree in business/marketing from the University of Southern California (USC), I possess a certificate from Robbins-Madanes Training-Life Coach Training, an online training institute founded by world-famous motivational speaker Tony Robbins and therapist Cloe Madanes. I completed the Robbins-Madanes Core 100 Training, which, to quote the program's online description, "contains four Mastery Units which focus on Megastrategies, Navigating Life Stages, Personal Transformation, and Key Decisions."

I selected the Robbins-Madanes program because I am an avid follower of Robbins, his principles, and philosophies. For those of you unaware of his work, Anthony "Tony" Robbins began his career at age 17 working for motivational speaker Jim Rohn. In the early 1980s, he began teaching neuro-linguistic programming and Ericksonian Hypnosis in partnership with American linguist, author, and management consultant John Grinder.

In 1988, Robbins released his first infomercial, *Personal Power*, establishing him as a noted "peak performance coach." Since then, he has published numerous best-selling books, including *Unlimited Power* (1986), *Awaken the Giant Within* (1991), *Unleash the Power Within* (1999), *Driving Force* (2005), and *Notes from a Friend* (2007). He has worked as a counselor for President Bill Clinton, hockey superstar Wayne Gretzky, tennis champion Serena Williams, Australian actor Hugh Jackman, and American businessmen Peter Guber, Steve Wynn, and Marc Benioff. *Accenture* named Robbins one of the Top 50 Business Intellectuals, and *Harvard Business Press* lists him among The Top 200 Business Gurus.

Robbins' style of psychoanalysis, dubbed "6 Human Needs" (Certainty, Variety, Significance, Love/Connection,

Growth and Contribution)—which he developed with Cloe Madanes—were instrumental in my own development, and responsible for much of my growth. To date, I have used his educational foundation, coupled with coping mechanisms and insight gleaned from a slew of sources—including Al-Anon and Eastern philosophy—to coach clients in many areas. My emphasis includes guidance regarding relationships, career, stress management, fear management, gender identity transition, and addiction (alongside professional resources).

At the end of the day, I have one simple message for all my clients: "I am not only your coach, but your advocate."

Creating BRAVE

Working with more than 50 clients during a four-year period led me to notice that most shared a common set of symptoms. Regardless of their social or economic status, they suffered from the same predicament. Similar to how I felt growing up, they experienced the pain of insecurity and anxiety.

If it had been years since they had addressed their problems, I also noticed a deep sense of pessimism—even despair. No matter if they were the successful company owners, business professionals, or stay-at-home parents, each tended to view the world as a hostile, unwelcoming place. Married, single, or divorced, they considered themselves inadequate and ill-prepared to take on life's challenges. They knew they needed to change but didn't know how to go about it.

Achieving this insight led me to develop a system by which my clients could learn to better face adversity with courage, confidence, and even optimism. Following its steps brought them comfort and relief. More importantly, it left them empowered with tools and knowhow to take life's everyday slings and arrows in stride. No longer so overwhelmed, they could focus on what makes them happy and life worth living.

I call my system BRAVE. In the course of developing it, I discovered several fundamental truths:

Starting over is healthy

How often have we wished we could wipe the record clean and begin again? Sometimes starting from scratch is not only desirable, but also necessary if we hope to move forward. Like a computer infected with viruses and malware over time, our minds can become clogged with malicious and self-destructive algorithms leading to pain and suffering, leaving a total "reboot"—or as close to one as we can achieve—the best option.

There is a value in personal development and self-actualization.

Too many people, perhaps *most* people, see themselves as finished projects rather than works in progress. We view our childhood and adolescence as the time for growth, education, and maturity, but for most us in adulthood it's a time to "settle down," "earn a living," and "raise a family." But as teachers are so fond of telling us, education is a lifetime adventure. It never stops. The same goes for personal development. When we are learning, growing, and changing, we are truly alive. And this is something we can do—something we *need* to do—literally until the day we die.

We can redesign/reframe relationships through mindful communication.

As with the particulars of our adult lives, we tend to view our personal relationships as static. We get frozen in our thinking. *We like the people we like. We hate the people we hate.* If we have a bad relationship with a family member or co-worker, that's the way it is.

If we've grown indifferent to our spouses, well, that's just the natural order of things, too. No sense in resisting the inevitable, right? In fact, nothing is further from the truth. We *can* change and improve our relationships, with friends, with family, with co-workers, just by changing the way we communicate, not to mention transforming our baseline thinking. Whether it be a strained relationship with an estranged parent, a hostile child, an irate employer, or an indifferent spouse, we can improve the status quo with a change in our perspective and our communication habits.

We must choose forgiveness over resentment.

We have all been wronged at some time in our lives. Our parents may have been less than ideal. Friends may have lied or taken advantage of us. Significant others may have betrayed or even abused us. A certain perverse satisfaction comes from memorializing these affronts and revisiting them in our minds, reveling in the pain the memories trigger much like we might play with a canker sore. But clinging to our bad memories can become poison, eating away at our emotional and physical health. Religious or not, we can take a page from the Bible: We must forgive those who trespass against us, just as we wish for them to forgive our trespasses. Nothing good comes from allowing wounds to fester.

We must exercise deeper compassion for others.

Empathy is a key component to the human psyche. Our ability to feel for others, to put ourselves in each other's shoes, is one of the fundamental pillars supporting human civilization. There isn't a religion on Earth that promotes selfishness, greed, and self-centeredness. And for good reason. By exercising compassion, we not only help build a safer, stronger, and more just society, we also elevate our own position within it.

We must live authentically within ourselves and the outside world.

Lies are destructive, none more so than the ones we tell ourselves. For much of human history, society valued conformity at all costs. Each sex filled prescribed roles. Men were breadwinners, warriors, scientists, and political leaders. Women were child-bearers, homemakers, nurses, and nurturers. Likewise, sexuality was constrained and regulated. Any deviation from established norms was considered not only abhorrent, but often criminal, sometimes punishable by death.

Only in recent decades have we come to recognize and understand how unnatural and destructive these restrictions are. Slowly, but inexorably, society is becoming more tolerant, even welcoming, of people whose inherent makeup dictates desires and behaviors skewing outside traditional norms. By accepting and celebrating our differences, we can finally live truly happy, fulfilled lives.

We must act from a solution-based, not problem-oriented, mindset.

Many people are naturally inclined to see the proverbial glass as half-empty rather than half-full. When problems arise, when events don't quite go as anticipated, they focus on the discomfort they're experiencing rather than looking for a way to alleviate it. The fact is, reality is indifferent to our plans and desires. Our complex, often chaotic universe doesn't consider our wishes or well-being as it goes about its business—and that's okay. As a result, we must be ready to face adversity whenever it rears its head and look for practical solutions rather than expend energy on placing blame, assigning guilt, or pining for "what might have been."

I honed my BRAVE system over several years by working with clients and evaluating its impact on their lives and sense of well-being. Clients who have used the BRAVE method have reported significant improvements in their situations and attitudes. The benefits they've reported include:

Enhanced self-esteem

BRAVE followers report they feel more confident, capable, worthy, and optimistic. They are also more willing to act on their beliefs, to stand up for their values, and accept risk.

Better able to cope with adversity.

Clients who employ the BRAVE method report they are better able to deal with negative news and events. They can take misfortunes in stride, adapt to change, and develop workable solutions to their problems.

Better able to achieve their goals.

The BRAVE system helps users focus on what is most meaningful to them, minimizing distractions, so they can reach their goals with less pain and effort.

The Tools You Will Acquire

This book contains a variety of tools you can use to improve all aspects of your life, including your career, relationships, and personal development. Let's now look at the system underlying it.

BRAVE stands for:

Benevoliefs

Benevolief is a term I coined to describe particularly helpful beliefs/assumptions. *They are benevolent self-beliefs.* If we are going to maximize our potential, we must begin by believing we *can.* (And stop being held hostage to limiting thoughts about ourselves and the world.) Choosing the right *benevolief* can get you off to a powerful start. As you will see with each of my case studies, I begin with the belief holding my client back, then transform it into a *benevolief* they can use to progress.

Readiness

In every classic 12-step program, the first step is to admit you have a problem. The BRAVE system similarly requires you to recognize the need for transformation and commit yourself to doing so *now.* Only when you are ready to change is transformation possible.

Alignment

To affect change, you must center yourself and account for all the factors impacting your negative behavior. Such preparation is akin to "getting all your ducks in a row," or knowing what you have to do and when you have to do it.

Vision

Vision means seeing your desired destination and the road to get there. It means creating a plan while viewing yourself honestly and compassionately.

Engagement

Once the plan has been created, it's time to take action. But action isn't a one-time thing. It's a process of action and reaction—learning from what works and what doesn't serve you.

Mastering the Three S's.

True application and success with the BRAVE system requires the recognition and analysis of three important psychological factors:

State of Mind

We must reflect on our current attitudes and dispositions *before* we can change them for the better. Rightly or wrongly, our moods and beliefs tend to be self-fulfilling. If we expect something to succeed, it increases the odds it will; conversely, if we expect something to fail, defeat becomes the more probable outcome.

Situation

We must understand the nature of the arena in which we play and our place within it. No one operates in a vacuum. We are all subject to many forces, including our social class, level of education, income bracket, and professional and social networks, as well as a wide variety of racial, ethnic, and sexual factors. All of these need to be assessed when making a viable life plan.

Status

Once we know where we are coming from, we need to take stock as to where we are along the path to our goal. Where do we want to be and how close are we to getting there? How much more distance needs to be covered before we can consider ourselves "successful"?

Additional Tools

At the end of each chapter you will find a series of additional tools you can use to help you on your journey to self-improvement. These include:

Exercises

I offer a series of mental and physical routines to help you sharpen your senses, memory, acuity, concentration, and understanding. Over time, these exercises will help put you in closer touch with your emotions, leading you to think in more positive, constructive ways.

Affirmations

The things we tell ourselves, both silently and aloud, impact how we feel and behave. Each chapter provides an affirmation that when stated and absorbed can put you in a more positive, action-oriented frame of mind.

Contemplations

Contemplation is a time-tested way to clear the mind and bring the body back into balance. At the end of each chapter, I present a contemplation to quiet troubling thoughts and foster greater understanding.

Communications Tools

Since childhood, we have learned many bad communication habits. These often result in misunderstandings, hurt feelings, and unnecessary power struggles. In each of the following chapters, I offer you alternative ways to communicate, promoting empathy, understanding, and cooperation.

Mindbreaking

The fact is, we can get caught up in negative forms of thinking. We can fall prey to limiting beliefs that imprison us in constrictive, restrictive patterns we don't ever feel we will be able to escape. In order to release ourselves from such limited thinking, we need to disrupt the status quo of our mind. We must *mindbreak to mindshift.*

Mindshifting

"*Mindshifting*" is one of the most important concepts in the BRAVE system. We have already talked about creating *benevoliefs*. This is how you get there. By changing old patterns of thinking that no longer serve you and constructing new paradigms of ideas, you can change the trajectory of your life. When this happens, the results can feel magical, almost miraculous. The truth is the effects are very real—and very achievable—once you reorient your thinking.

In this book, I will show you how to combine *mindbreaking* and *mindshifting* with the five principles of BRAVE to create a blueprint for a more satisfying and fulfilling life. But first we need to be realistic with ourselves and understand what's possible. Magical thinking does us no good; neither does skimping on the hard, inner work.

BRAVE is not a Magic Bullet

Speaking of inner work, the secret to BRAVE rests on one core principle: No matter what's going on in your life, the key to dealing with it is doing the inner work. How often have we heard the phrase, "You can't change someone else?" There's much truth to it. You often can't change another person, nor should you even try. What you *can* do—*what's in your power*—is change yourself, starting with *mindshifting*.

BRAVE may be a powerful system for self-improvement, but it is no magic bullet. Just reading this book won't make your problems vanish like the morning fog, send you into a state of exuberant euphoria, make you irresistible to the opposite sex, rid you of a lifetime of emotional baggage, or even allow you to lose those stubborn last five pounds. Like anything useful, BRAVE takes time and effort to work. The more you put into it, the more you'll get out of it.

When using the BRAVE system, results vary by individual. Some people report seeing results quickly, often within just a matter of days. For others, it can take weeks or even months before they see measurable progress. And, alas, for a small percentage of people, their situation is so dire that even this powerful system cannot provide the necessary help. (I would be less than forthright if I didn't acknowledge this last point. There are problems beyond my scope, requiring medical intervention. If and when these arise in my practice, I refer these to the appropriate professionals.)

What's Possible

Knowing that true mastery and self-transformation is a work in progress demanding self-sacrifice and commitment, what can you expect from the process? At minimum, using the BRAVE system will point you in the right direction. You will begin to wean yourself away from negative habits and embrace more helpful, constructive thoughts and thoughts and behaviors. You may find yourself a little happier. A little more alert. A little more focused. A little more able to enjoy life's pleasures.

At best, following BRAVE can change your life for the better. You may find yourself taking on greater risks and challenges than you would have ever before considered. You may find yourself enjoying activities you previously rejected. You may find your home life is more stable, more satisfying, and more rewarding. You may find yourself performing better at work, achieving goals, and receiving recognition faster and with less effort. You also may find yourself facing the future with previously unexperienced levels of hope and optimism.

How this Book is Written

This is not your standard "how-to" book. Each chapter contains three parts:

Biography

The first section of each chapter contains a portion of my life story, offering insights into how I came to discover, develop, and implement the BRAVE system. I do this to illustrate that BRAVE is not the result of some academic exercise or detached professional analysis, but grew out of profound personal experiences. I believe that, like any good life story, my biography is both specific and universal. In the following chapters, I will introduce you to an America as viewed through the lens of a first-generation Indian-American woman and share with you experiences, joys, and traumas that no doubt echo those you, too, have undergone.

Case Studies

In each chapter, I share stories of how my clients have used the BRAVE system to cope with adversity, handle long-standing emotional issues, and improve their lives through changes in attitude and behavior. (I edited their names and identifying characteristics, of course, for the sake of confidentiality.) Innumerable studies have shown, and I concur, that storytelling is an effective way to share information. I believe you will find these true-life case studies fascinating, informative, edifying, and inspirational.

Exercises

Here is where we put the BRAVE system into practice. I will show you how to acquire the skills you need to follow BRAVE at home, at work, and at play. Follow these exercises as described and you will likely see improvements in your attitude and life's performance. As I said earlier, when we change our thinking, everything else changes. If you reframe the things you fear using the ideas described in this book, you can indeed lead a more productive, fulfilling life.

Mindset is a Choice

We all have many reasons not to be brave. We may not have been born into wealth and privilege. We may have been raised by single parents, relatives, by foster parents, or even in orphanages. We may not have genius-level intellects or natural talents for music, art, business, or sports. We may not be conventionally beautiful or handsome or charming. Our sexuality may not naturally conform to social norms. We may be handicapped by physical or mental deficits, inborn or acquired. We may have suffered physical or emotional traumas at the hands of strangers or those we trusted. We may have suffered the sudden loss of loved ones as the result of illness or misfortune. We may have been ostracized by our peers due to our skin color, our accent, our religion, our weight, our way of speaking, or our sexual orientation. We may simply be the victims of a negative mindset.

While none of these factors should be discounted, none present insurmountable barriers to happiness and success. With the right tools, attitude, and commitment, any adversity can be overcome. If you are ready to change your life, take the first step with me by experiencing the story of Anastasia, my client. She, too, had to learn to be BRAVE to obtain what she desired.

Case Study: Anastasia

Anastasia is a 49-year-old Indian-American woman born in Los Angeles, California, and now living in L.A. where she works as a property manager. She has never married and has no children.

By the time she became my client, Anastasia had already survived an eating disorder, methamphetamine and gambling addictions, had been briefly homeless, and had also served jail time for drug possession. She had turned her life around with the help of Alcoholics Anonymous (AA) and support of family and friends, as well as professional therapy. Ultimately, she had obtained a Ph.D. in psychology.

Yet, despite her successes, she found herself gripped by depression and unable to focus on what she desired from her career. She felt aimless, powerless, and hopeless.

State of Mind

Anastasia felt confused about her career path. Like many people, she didn't believe she had many options, and those she had she feared would not lead to personal fulfillment. She viewed the world and her life in stark, negative terms.

Situation

She was working full-time as a property manager for a real estate company in Los Angeles. She wanted to set new goals, improve her sense of motivation, and become healthier, both physically and emotionally.

Status

Anastasia wanted to ensure her life unfolded in a positive direction. She also wanted to manage the demons that seemed to bring her back to old, destructive behaviors. We addressed this particular challenge through visualization techniques, leading her to replace older, dysfunctional habits.

Being BRAVE

Beliefs >>> *Benevoliefs* (Show-Stopping Eyes):

Belief: "I cannot see a way forward in my career."

Benevolief: "I can see my future clearly and am ready to start a heroic journey to achieve my goals."

Readiness (I Can See Clearly):

I used "creative visualization" to help Anastasia deal with her negative coping mechanisms. After getting her to relax, I asked her to picture herself as a bubblehead octopus, a metaphor for her head filled with useless and negative emotions. I then asked her to visual herself using her multiple arms to keep these emotions at bay.

Alignment (Inner Beauty):

Anastasia told me physical exercise always gives her strength and energy. I therefore recommended she work out for 30 minutes a day, five days a week. This could take the form of running, speed walking, weightlifting, or aerobics. She also said she had a junk food addiction she wanted to break. Specifically, she loved hot Cheetos, and could easily consume an entire bag in a single sitting. To help her overcome this, I offered two options:

1. For one day, she could eat as many hot Cheetos as she wished. She could pretend she was going for a "personal record" in this category. I instructed her to write down how she felt at the end of her binge.
2. She could replace her hot Cheetos habit with another, healthier compulsion. She could practice making hard choices, easing the strain with the knowledge she would benefit from the results.

Ultimately, she chose Option #2, replacing hot Cheetos with olives and crackers, a snack she would reward herself with after walking 30 minutes daily. Finally, I recommended books and articles on self-awareness she could read or listen to during her exercise periods.

Vision (Enjoying the Ride):

I asked Anastasia to visualize herself as a feminine warrior: tall, strong, confident, and capable. She was a commander, self-motivated and able to take on any foe or obstacle. Her great strength was equaled only by her great heart, as she was able to show great compassion to others as well as to herself.

Engagement (Taking On My Own Case):

Using an internal analysis technique, I had Anastasia replace her ongoing internal conversations around guilt and fear with affirmations promoting motivation and gentleness.

Outcomes

Anastasia has put my suggestions into practice and reported feeling measurably better about herself and her prospects. She says she has become more cognizant of her behaviors by approaching them with increased self-awareness and insight.

She still works in property management and continues to pursue her goals on the side. Her diet has improved markedly, and she continues to replace her negative mantras with more positive affirmations, making her receptive to new relationships and healthy lifestyle changes.

What I Learned from This Client

Working with Anastasia, I was reminded to be compassionate with myself and to use self-care to deal with my own challenges. From her example, I learned it takes strength to move out of my comfort zone and say "no" to enticing, but ultimately damaging, compulsions. I celebrate opportunities like this in which I can be around other women I can be proud of.

For Contemplation: What did you learn from the adults in your childhood about being brave? Do you remember what you thought "brave" meant?

Affirmation: *"I choose to bravely make changes in my life."*

Exercise: Start a journal to make notes of thoughts and ideas that come up for you as you read this book. At minimum, each day write down three things for which you are grateful.

Chapter 2
Being Brave as a Lion

The Metaphor of the Lion

For thousands of years, the lion has been a symbol of bravery, pride, and royalty throughout the African and Eurasian continents. Although we now think of lions as denizens of sub-Saharan Africa, these majestic apex predators once roamed as far north as central Europe and as far east as India. Feared and respected for their size, strength, and ferocity, these magnificent felines have become synonymous with royalty, leadership, and martial power.

Approximately 17,000 years ago, Paleolithic humans in the caves of Lascaux and Chauvet, France, painted the first known depictions of lions. The ancient Egyptians depicted many of their war gods as lions, including the eternal sphinx. The ancient Sumerians, Assyrians, and Babylonians all used lion symbols to denote royalty. Many of Aesop's Fables featured lions, and the Greek demigod Hercules famously slew the Nemean lion and wore its skin to symbolize victory over death. Many European monarchs added some form of "lion" to their monikers to elevate their status, most famously King Richard the Lionheart of England, Henry the Lion of Germany, and William the Lion of Scotland. Today, lion symbols adorn the flags of such nations as Bermuda, the Cayman Islands, Montenegro, Spain, and Sri Lanka, as well as the regional flags of Scotland, Macedonia, Flanders, and Bavaria.

Lions also prominently appear in popular culture. Leo the Lion is one of our 12 symbols of the zodiac. The Detroit Lions are one of the NFL's most enduring franchises. MGM has used the lion as its symbol since the studio's founding in 1924. And anthropomorphized lions are key characters in everything from L. Frank Baum's *The Wonderful Wizard of Oz* to C.S. Lewis's Narnia series to Disney's *The Lion King.*

In my own Indian culture, the Hindu warrior goddess Durga looms large as one of the most powerful and enduring mythological characters. Her name has been translated at different times as "impassable," "invincible" or "unassailable." Traditionally depicted riding a lion, her multiple arms sport a variety of weapons, including a chakra, a conch, a bow and arrow, javelin, and shield. Despite her fearsome power, her expression is always depicted as calm and serene. This is because Durga does not fight out of rage, hatred, or blood-lust, but because it is her solemn duty to protect the world from evil. She is a willing champion of the weak, the downtrodden, and the oppressed.

Critical to understanding Durga is her symbiotic relationship with the lion she rides. The two are always seen as one. *They function as one.* The warrior is the lion. The lion is the warrior. Together they are fearless and undefeatable.

The metaphor of the lion—and of Durga—offers an apt description of *mindshifting,* of learning to be brave. Being brave requires us to not only be strong and capable, but also calm and resolute. We must be confident in our own power and fearless against those circumstances or people challenging us and our sovereignty. Or as Durga might suggest: Keep the image of the lion in your mind as you strut and roar and you will become ruler of your own jungle.

BRAVE's Meaning and Significance

As stated in Chapter 1, BRAVE is my acronym for Beliefs to *Benevoliefs,* Readiness, Alignment, Vision and Engagement. But this acronym also intentionally conveys its literal meaning, "possessing or exhibiting courage or courageous endurance." When we contemplate bravery, certain stock images come to mind.

We might think of the classic cleft-chinned knight in shining armor facing off against a monstrous fire-breathing dragon. We might imagine a soldier fearlessly sprinting across no-man's-land to take out an enemy machine gun nest, with bullets and shells exploding all around. We might think of a police officer climbing onto a ledge 10 stories high to talk down a would-be suicide, or a firefighter rushing into a burning building to save a trapped child from burning upper floor apartment. We might also think of a mountain climber scaling a sheer cliff side, or an unknown Chinese dissident facing down a column of tanks in Beijing's Tiananmen Square.

But one does not have to be a warrior to be brave. One need not face physical peril or risk substantial personal loss in pursuit of some noble goal to demonstrate courage. Bravery can be found everywhere. At work. At home. In the public square. It can be practiced in our relationships, in our professional behavior, and in our life choices. True bravery means *mindshifting* and can encompass many things, including:

Getting out of your comfort zone

This has always been a source of stress for me personally, and I suspect it is probably one for you as well. We like the things we are accustomed to and fear the unknown. To be brave means to venture beyond the tried and true, to be open to new experiences, new people, and new ideas.

Changing your old paradigm

Most of us hold beliefs, values, and habits we can trace back to our childhoods. While a strong set of core values is a necessary foundation for a happy life, much of what we believe to be true is not always correct. We must *mindbreak* by questioning our most basic assumptions, to separate fact from conjecture, values from prejudices, and natural limits from self-imposed constraints.

Recognizing the influences that have shaped your life

None of us are truly "self-made." We are the products of a vast number of influences molding and shaping our psyches. Some of these influences include our parents, our teachers, our religious faith, our friends and acquaintances, and the media. Understanding where we acquire our thoughts and feelings is a good first step toward *mindbreaking* from old paradigms and fashioning a philosophy better serving us as evolving individuals.

Learning to control your emotions

More often than not, our behavior is guided by our feelings. Whether it be positive emotions, like love, joy, curiosity, or altruism, or negative emotions like fear, hate, jealousy, or rage, we act on feelings far more often than responding through cold, rational analysis. Unfortunately, our habit of giving into emotional-based compulsions can lead us into dark and dangerous territory. It's often said bravery isn't the lack of fear, but the ability to overcome it; being able to do the right thing even when we know such an action to be uncomfortable or even downright painful. Bravery means learning how to rule from our head *and* heart instead of just our guts.

Being open to new solutions

The older we get, the more we cling to the familiar and conventional. At a certain point in life, too many of us decide we have "figured it all out" and there is nothing more to learn. At least nothing of value. But we can't improve ourselves if we're not open to new ideas and ways of doing things. We must see ourselves as works in progress until the day we die.

Accepting your authentic self

This can be the most difficult and painful task of all. Most of us are desperate to live up to other people's expectations. We want to please our parents. Our spouses. Our children. We long to be the person others want us to be. But this is not always possible. Nor even advisable. To be truly BRAVE is to find your true inner self and bring it to the surface—to live the life that makes you happy and unfilled—regardless of your family or society's judgments.

The Source for My Ideas

Like you, I am the product of numerous influences I encountered as a child and later as an adult. I acquired many ideas passively from influencers, such as my parents, my teachers, my siblings, and my religious instructors. I did not seek these people out; I was placed under their influence by either the unique circumstances of my birth, my parents' efforts, or the public-school system. Later, as my eyes opened to a wider world and I grew capable of thinking for myself, I began proactively seeking life's answers from a wide variety of sources. These include:

Authors' Self-Actualization Books and Systems

In Chapter 1, I briefly mentioned my affinity for motivational speaker Tony Robbins and his extensive writings on self-improvement. Other modern authors who have impressed me include:

Alan W. Watts (*The Wisdom of Insecurity: A Message for an age of Anxiety*)

Al-Anon B-16 (*Courage to Change*)

Angela Duckworth (*GRIT - The Power of Passion and Perseverance*)

Tony Robbins (*Unlimited Power, Awaken the Giant Within, etc.*)

Daniel Goleman (*Emotional Intelligence*)

Malcolm Gladwell (*Blink, Outliers*, etc.)

Paramahansa Yogananda (*Autobiography of a Yogi*)

Sidney Rosen (*My Voice Will Go With You: The Teaching Tales of Milton H. Erickson*)

T.D. Jakes (*Instinct*)

(At the end of this book, I will offer a more complete recommended reading list, expanding on these titles.)

12-Step Programs

Bill Wilson and Dr. Robert Holbrook founded Alcoholics Anonymous (AA), the first 12-step program, in 1935. Since then, hundreds of programs have been established following the AA model to help people deal with pathologies ranging from gambling addiction to narcotics abuse. In fact, the third-largest 12-step program, Al-Anon (which we will later discuss), uses similar methods to help not addicts, but their suffering families, friends, and loved ones.

The crux of all 12-step programs revolves around the belief that recovery requires a three-pronged approach: physical, mental, and spiritual, and that support from others dealing with the same affliction is critical to long-term success. I have found the non-judgmental nature of these programs and their emphasis on improving interpersonal communication to be powerful and useful to even non-addicts pursuing personal improvement.

Spiritual Thinkers

Numerous spiritual thinkers have contributed to my personal philosophy. These include:

Paramahansa Yogananda
His quest for life's meaning.

Mahatma Gandhi
His grace and message on non-violence.

Alan Watts
His philosophy, merging Eastern and Western ideas.

Sri Jayendra Puri Swamiji
His teaching of personal faith to me directly.

Religious Traditions

As an Indian-American raised in late 20th century suburbia, I have been exposed to numerous religions, and have tried to absorb the best of each. These include:

Jainism

The religion of my birth, Jainism (traditionally known as *Jain Dharma*) is an ancient Indian religion whose origins date back more than 2,500 years. Followers of Jainism are called "Jains," a word derived from the Sanskrit word *jina,* which describes a path of ethical and spiritual refinement one must follow to move beyond the cycle of birth and rebirth. The main premises of Jainism are:

Ahimsa – Non-violence

Anekantavada – Many-sidedness

Aparigraha – Non-attachment

Asceticism – Avoidance of sensual pleasures

Jainists also believe in the Hindu principles called the Purusarthas. They are:

Dharma. This involves ethical behavior and "doing one's duty."

Artha. This involves the acquisition of material wealth through constructive work as well as public service.

Moksha. The focus on spiritual elevation through meditation and liberation.

Like Hindus, and its spiritual offshoot, Buddhism, Jainists believe in karma. The concept is that future outcomes result from present-day actions. In other words, "what goes around comes around."

Christianity

Raised in Southern California, I couldn't help but be exposed to the majority-Christian faith of the area and absorb many of its ideas. Of these, I continue to find the concepts of forgiveness and redemption—the idea we can all be "saved" by changing our attitudes and behaviors from negative to positive—the most compelling. Too often, people believe their negative behaviors have dug them into a hole so deep they can never escape. Christianity teaches otherwise; through faith, hope, and good works, even the most "lost" among us can turn our lives around.

Judaism

Over the years, I have examined the teachings of the Old Testament as well as how this ancient Middle Eastern religion is practiced in America today. First and foremost, I have learned Judaism is based on the idea of "law," on doing the right thing not in the hope of achieving rewards in some abstract afterlife, but to make the world better here and now. Its philosophy has always been one of questioning, inquiry, and healthy skepticism. This is why classical Judaism reveres nothing more than scholarly pursuits. (Something that resonates with me.)

Thoughts on Emotional Intelligence

Now that you understand the basis for my ideas, I would like to turn our discussion to one of the key areas of my practice, a realm highly informed by the influences of my past and yet constantly evolving. In my work as a life coach, I have found that, more than anything else, possessing a high level of emotional intelligence is critical to leading a successful life, both personally and professionally. The fiercest, bravest people I've ever known were also the most emotionally advanced.

So, *what is emotional intelligence?* Emotional intelligence is generally defined as the ability to identify your emotions, control them, and understand and respond to others' feelings. Even though the term E.Q. has gained in popularity (as in Emotional Quotient, akin to IQ), there is no scientifically standardized test for it, leading some scholars to claim such a thing does not even exist. But as any adult with life experience knows, some people are far better at controlling their emotions than others. Likewise, some people can "read" other people well. And of course, some individuals have a hard time connecting on an emotional level.

At a certain point in our lives, we've likely encountered a person we just naturally vibe with. It's not unusual to discover this same individual has a sprawling social network, and seems to be everybody's best friend. This person often wears an easy smile, greets you with a firm handshake, and shows a keen interest in whatever others have to say. On the other hand, we've also known "cold fish," standoffish folks who tend to say the wrong thing at the wrong time, and even regard others' mere presence as an annoyance.

There is little link between what experts call general intelligence, which is measured by the IQ test, and emotional intelligence. *The Big Bang Theory's* Sheldon Cooper stereotype is often celebrated as the standard for a smart person. For whatever reason, popular culture seems to think genius and emotional disconnection go hand in hand, but this isn't true. Many intelligent people are also highly emotionally intelligent. Rhodes Scholar and former President Bill Clinton was famous for his ability to connect with diverse groups of people on a deep emotional level. His "I feel your pain" line became a well-known catch phrase. Moreover, there are many who succeed in life despite having merely average intelligence just because of their innate ability to empathize and bond with those around them.

So, what does emotional intelligence look like in practice? In his book *EQ, Applied,* psychologist Justin Bariso describes 13 ways that individuals with this skillset behave:

They think about their emotions

People with high emotional intelligence are aware of how they feel and how their emotions impact their behavior.

They think before they act...or speak

Aware that emotional compulsions can be dangerous, those with high EQ often pause before acting or reacting.

They work to control their thoughts

They try not to let their feelings govern their thinking. Few people can turn their emotions on and off, but those with high EQ can set their feelings aside to think and act in a more rational manner.

They benefit from criticism

People with high emotional intelligence welcome constructive criticism and use it to improve themselves. Even when criticism seems unwarranted, the high EQ individual might ask, *"Why did the person react this way?"* and attempt to diffuse or improve the situation.

They're authentic

In his classic 1951 novel, *The Catcher in the Rye,* author J.D. Salinger uses his hero Holden Caulfield to rail against "fakes and phonies," people who would say and do anything just to get on your good side or establish dominance over you. People with high EQ don't bare their souls at every encounter, but they do act in accordance with a firm set of values, standards, and principles.

They demonstrate empathy

Empathy is not the same as sympathy. Sympathetic people feel *for* other people. Empathetic people feel *with* other people. They may not always agree with someone's position or reaction, but they're capable of understanding the feelings behind it.

They praise others

Quick to acknowledge the good works of others, they understand the value of being appreciated.

They give helpful feedback

Because they welcome constructive input—and know how devastating negative comments can be—high EQ individuals are careful to frame their own criticism in positive, helpful ways.

They apologize

Saying "I'm sorry" can be a difficult thing to do but people with high EQ are not afraid to acknowledge when they have done something wrong. They also understand that even when they're not wrong, apologizing can be a powerful way to build emotional bridges and stronger relationships.

They forgive and forget

Holding grudges is never useful. A grudge is like a wound allowed to fester and spread, ultimately leading to permanent injury. Better to learn to manage hurt feelings and move on.

They keep their promises

Setting someone up and then letting them down is hurtful and callous. People with high emotional intelligence are aware of how their actions impact others and do everything possible to keep their commitments.

They help others

People with high EQ are eager to provide any assistance they can, even if it's just giving advice or support.

They're sensitive to emotional manipulation

Being aware of their emotions and empathetic to those of others, people with high EQ are quick to recognize when someone is attempting to use emotions or emotional appeals to manipulate them. As much as high EQ individuals use their sensitivities to help others, they also use them to protect themselves from those who would do them harm.

EQ: BRAVERY's Secret Weapon

So why is emotional intelligence important for self-improvement? For one, if your goal is to feel better—to show up bravely in life—you need to know *how* you feel currently and *why* you feel the way you do. Also, in the vast majority of cases, feeling better involves breaking out of your own emotional bubble, reaching out, and connecting with others. The sharper your emotional intelligence, the easier and more effective this becomes.

So how do you become more emotionally intelligent? Unlike general intelligence, which tends to have strong genetic underpinnings, emotional intelligence is something that can be cultivated and improved. Basically, it's within your power. But first, you have to practice. Life offers no shortage of opportunities to slow down, to look inward when unruly feelings grip you, compelling you to act without thinking. One good way to develop EQ is to become more mindful in the moment. Before taking any significant action, ask yourself, "Why am I doing this? What am I feeling? Is my response appropriate to the situation? Is there a chance I'll be doing myself more harm than good?"

Another way to hone your EQ skills is to practice empathy. For instance, when dealing with people in extreme emotional states, try to imagine yourself in their positions. If someone is acting in ways you find objectionable or offensive, ask yourself, "Why are they doing this? What might they be feeling? How have I acted and/or reacted under similar circumstances?" Thinking along these lines will allow you to build that heart/mind connection we discussed. By practicing empathy, we not only create bridges between ourselves and others, we also gain firmer control over our own emotional states for greater success in life.

Your Personal BRAVERY Toolbox

A number of time-tested tools can help in our quest for personal growth and improvement. Certainly, not all of them offer the same efficacy; however, simply being aware of these tools and what they can do for you will allow you to show up in braver ways, no matter what life throws at you.

Meditation:

Meditation and meditative prayer are common practices in many spiritual traditions, including Judaism, Christianity, Islam, Hinduism, Buddhism, and Taoism. Defined simply, meditation is the practice of clearing the mind of extraneous thoughts and emotions by focusing all of one's attention on one's inner being. This is a relatively simple skill to acquire, but it does take some time to master. (Holding focus is not nearly as easy as you might suspect.)

Many scientific researchers have studied the biology of meditation and discovered strong links between the practice and positive health outcomes. Among other benefits, it appears to be an effective way to reduce stress, lower blood pressure, inhibit inflammation, promote restful sleep, and fight depression. More importantly, meditation allows you to reduce limiting beliefs, opening up spaces for *benevoliefs.*

Mindfulness:

Related to meditation, this practice involves focusing one's attention on the moment. A significant difference between the two is that while meditation traditionally requires one to sit still and be quiet for long periods of time, mindfulness can be practiced under any condition, even seemingly chaotic ones necessitating bravery, such as physical combat.

Drawing on the fundamentals of EQ, mindfulness requires one to think in the present, to be aware of what is happening to one's body, to acknowledge, but not be overwhelmed by, one's emotions, and to consciously link one's feelings with one's thoughts. As noted above, mindfulness can be particularly useful in times of high stress; combat pilots, for example, need razor-sharp concentration so they can act and react to rapidly changing threats and conditions within fractions of a second. Martial arts combat, fencing, and similar contact sports require similarly high degrees of mindfulness.

Creative Visualization:

Unlike meditation or mindfulness—although again somewhat related—creative visualization involves preparing the mind and body for action by first imagining, in as vivid detail as possible, the result one wants to achieve. Many champion athletes use creative visualization to prepare themselves for upcoming competitions, repeatedly "seeing" themselves throwing the winning touchdown, making the record-setting long jump, or beating their rival runners. Such prophesies then become self-fulfilling. This same technique can be used to help achieve any number of difficult goals, be it finishing a creative project or breaking an addiction, particularly through use of vision and engagement, both important parts of the BRAVE system.

Wellness:

As we all know, the mind and body are intimately connected. Therefore, for the mind to function at peak capacity, the body must be equally optimized. Achieving wellness involves proper diet, regular exercise, sufficient sleep time, and attention to overall healthcare, including managing body weight, blood pressure, cholesterol, blood sugar, and related health markers.

Affirmations:

Affirmations are simple, positive statements we tell ourselves to ready and align ourselves in a positive state of mind, bolstering our self-confidence, and helping us overcome life's inevitable setbacks. I offer several affirmations throughout this book. When creating your own affirmation, you should write it down in present tense, as though you already have the quality you are affirming (e.g. "I always finish what I start.")

You should also repeat the affirmation throughout the day, use it as a mantra, in meditation, or as a writing prompt. Try saying it into a mirror and posting it throughout your home in places where you will see the affirmation. Repetition is the key. The more the mind encounters a thought, the more likely it is to make it a reality.

Journaling:

Consider allotting a few minutes each day to writing down your thoughts and feelings. I suggest using free-writing techniques; putting down whatever happens to be on your mind at the moment. Don't worry about spelling, grammar, or punctuation, and avoid censoring yourself. Part of the journal should focus on gratitude, as like attracts like. When you write about the things you're thankful for, the things that make you happy you tend to bring more of them into your life.

Mentors, Guides, and Coaches:

If possible, seek the support of a mentor, guide, or coach, someone you respect who can provide guidance and support in your personal journey. Being BRAVE doesn't necessarily mean going it alone. Having a support system in place can be very helpful, especially when you encounter roadblocks or enter new, unfamiliar territory.

Before concluding this chapter, let's turn our attention to a story exemplifying the spirit of the lion in action. The following teaches us bravery often means rising to challenges testing our very limits. By employing EQ—by being strong in our heart and mind—we can rise above the fray and stay unconquered.

Case Study: LaPressa - 48-Year-Old Female

LaPressa is biologically female, but sees herself as male (at times). She has a strong, bold, and confident Type-A personality.

State of Mind

She doesn't fully accept her masculine side and has consciously suppressed it, fearing she may be misunderstood or, worse, her loved ones may reject her. Her inner gender conflict causes her to mistrust others and distracts her from thriving in business.

Situation

LaPressa is confused. She wants to embrace her masculine side but doesn't want to make a physical change. She doesn't know if she can look like a woman but behave like a man.

Status

She cannot yet acknowledge her inner truth for fear of encountering hostility from others. She cannot trust others, or properly manage her wellness business.

LaPressa's Statements:

"I was born a biological female, but when I look in a mirror, I see a man (at times) Noticing my reflection, I can see my right side is distorted; it looks ugly because it looks masculine. On my left side, I see a girl. My goal is to accept my right side and make friends with it."

"What to do I look like to other people? I get mixed messages. My sister always made fun of the way I photographed. Like there was something wrong with me."

"I've had these feelings since childhood. I have always had a masculine temperament; I always wanted to be in the one in charge. I always knew what I wanted to accomplish, how I wanted to do things, and always wanted to be in the driver's seat."

"My sexual awakening occurred early; I believe I was around 5 at the time. I found it very confusing. As a result, I became very aggressive."

"By the time I was a teenager, my parents had divorced and my mother remarried. I was molested by my stepfather, and my mother knew about it. One day, I had enough. I stood up for myself in front of them. I said I would no longer put up with my stepdad's behavior. This triggered a big fight. They threw me out of the house and I had to move in with my grandparents. My grandfather was a good man, but always angry. Retired, he spent most of his waking hours camped out in front of the TV."

"I never had a strong male figure in my life. I did have an older brother and a younger brother, but neither filled this role. As a result, I became my own 'male' role model. I liked that part of myself. I called him 'Randy' (a character from the movie *Little Darlings*) and saw him as tough. I instigated fights with my classmates and always strutted around with a 'Don't mess with me' attitude.

"Maybe I had to do this to survive. I grew up in chaos. My neighborhood was gang-infested and violence erupted on a daily basis. I was this white kid—a girl—trapped in an environment I could not escape. My only choice was to become as tough as the world around me."

"I have to work to control my emotions. As a child, I was very emotional—what you might call a 'crybaby' and frequently criticized for emotional outbursts. They called me a drama queen. This emotionalism led me to sabotage my relationships with men and lose platonic friendships as well."

"I stopped wearing makeup when I got out of high school. I was fed up with trying to look feminine. Lately, I have been exposing my masculine side to my female friends. I like to say I must have been a gay man in a previous life. When I hang around with my friends, I get to be the man."

"My fantasy role model is Wonder Woman. Not for her appearance, but for her strength and confidence."

When I last met LaPressa, she wore an arrowhead around her neck. She explained this was a symbol of a warrior. She believed she may have been a Cree Indian in a past life.

Being BRAVE

Beliefs >>> *Benevoliefs* (Respect for Randy).

In working with LaPressa, I knew we had to *mindbreak* from harmful assumptions and *mindshift* to more constructive positions. To *mindbreak*, LaPressa needed to come to grips with what wasn't in her life. *Mindshifting* meant creating a new and gentle awareness and acceptance around her "Randy" personality. It was my hope that one day LaPressa could be comfortable expressing her emotional truth.

In service of this aspiration, I recommended LaPressa pay attention to her masculine feelings as they arose, trusting "Randy" to assume control of her behavior during times of stress. I advised her to use a journal to document her feelings about "Randy" on a daily basis to form a friendship with this aspect of her personality.

Readiness: Family Forgiveness

I recommended LaPressa reconsider her relationship with her mother and how she felt about growing up. It was critical LaPressa *mindshift* in regard to her mother to begin the forgiveness process. Yes, her mom may not have given her the emotional support she needed as a child, but LaPressa is now an adult and no longer requires this kind of parenting.

Together, we worked on the meanings of true compassion and empathy. Only by putting this into regular practice could LaPressa evolve her EQ, leading to success in all areas of her life. LaPressa accepted this challenge and began working on new thought processes she could employ during her next family reunion (an event sure to stir up challenging feelings).

Alignment: Business Venture

LaPressa decided to dissolve her business partnership because she and her partner did not share the same vision and values. This choice was a difficult one but she ultimately concluded she did not fully trust her partner and thus the business arrangement needed to end. She now operates the business as a sole proprietorship. In our discussions, LaPressa noted that her new *benevolief* helped her keep focus, assume the risks she was facing, and rebuild her wellness business in line with her personal goals.

Vision: Business Plan

LaPressa bravely approached her new role with both fear and excitement. Together, we laid out the steps she would need to take to start her wellness business (which had a strong focus on massage therapy).

These steps included:

- **Developing a business plan.**

- **Creating a savings plan.**

- **Temporarily working in a center with other specialists until she could afford to get a space of her own.**

- **Generating and implementing a branding strategy.**

- **Growing her client base.**

LaPressa is a natural healer, and I wanted her to see herself in that role. Healing was to be not only her profession, but her mission. It was to be manifested in every aspect of her life.

Engage: Cree Empowerment

LaPressa needed to practice mindfulness and clear her brain of clutter. I recommended regular *mindbreaks*, consisting of taking three deep breaths with her shoulders up, then slowly exhaling with her shoulders down while chanting the word "Cree."

(As noted earlier, LaPressa believed she is the reincarnation of a Cree Indian and drew strength from identifying with this heroic archetype.)

During this exercise, I asked her to imagine herself as a warrior, someone of great strength, confidence, and bravery. These techniques have become her new anchors and have lessened the stressful aspects of her emotional triggers.

For Contemplation:

Lions navigate through their instincts, allowing their feelings to dictate their next actions and plans. How can a change within align you to a new level of courage?

Affirmation:

"Wonder Woman first arms her internal powers before exhibiting them on to others. This is beauty exuded."

Exercise:

Ask yourself, what is your personal barometer of self-confidence, both internally and externally? Create a scale of 1 to 5. Create two such barometers. On the first list, include those internal/character attributes you feel are most important (e.g., being thoughtful, empathetic, forgiving, trustworthy, honest, etc.) When it comes to the other barometer, list those attributes you want to show the outside world (e.g., being physically strong and healthy, having a great smile, dressing well, etc.). Now rate yourself on each scale.

If you're like most people, you won't see yourself as a "5" anywhere on the list. This is okay. We all have room for improvement. Now, next to each attribute, write a way you can improve that particular quality, beginning with "Bravely …" (Example: If you want to be physically healthy, you might write "Bravely avoiding sugars and processed foods.") This way, you can establish specific goals and identify equally specific ways to achieve them. Adding "Bravely" to your action list helps focus your mind, making it part of a formal, organized self-improvement program.

Chapter 3
How My Childhood Taught Me Not to Be Brave

Nature vs. Nurture

For centuries, biologists, psychologists, sociologists, and philosophers have debated the question: From where does character and behavior spring? One's own biology or the environment? Is it internal or external? Nature or nurture? In fact, the alliterative phrase "nature versus nurture" goes all the way back to Elizabethan times. An even older variation can be found in medieval French. Its modern meaning was popularized by the 19th century scientist Francis Galton, a half-cousin of Charles Darwin, whose belief in the power of biological pre-programming led to him found the fields of eugenics (the selective breeding of humans) and behavioral genetics (how inheritance influences personality and behavior.)

Over the past 100 years, increasingly sophisticated studies have shed light on the role heredity and upbringing play in our lives. The discovery of DNA in the early 20th century, the identification of its double-helix structure by James Watson and Francis Crick in 1953, and the mapping of the human genome, completed in 2003, have led to amazing discoveries as to the role heredity plays in our in daily lives and our destinies. The general consensus holds that *both* nature and nurture are influential; each tends to affect the other over time.

It turns out aspects of our personalities are far more influenced by genetics than we might realize. For instance, your religion, or lack of one, is mostly dependent on your upbringing. No one is born a Christian or a Hindu or even an atheist. (Because of Judaism's unique nature, one can say that one is "born" Jewish in terms of bloodline, but certainly not in terms of specific religious beliefs.)

However, the likelihood you will actually *embrace* the religion you are taught, or any religion at all, appears to be largely influenced by certain genetic factors. You can be dragged to church every Sunday, be bar-mitzvah'ed, or kneel on a prayer rug facing Mecca five times daily, but if you don't have the "God" gene, it's just not going to stick. Religion is learned, but *religiosity* appears to be biologically innate.

So far, we have talked a lot about empathy; this is another quality impacted by genetics. Ask any parent and they will tell you that kids have a tendency to be self-centered. It's not necessarily a bad thing, it's just a fact of life that part of raising a child involves helping them see things from another's point of view—offering perspective and helping them to take another's feelings into consideration. Most of us acquire these abilities over time. We learn empathy is instrumental in creating long-standing, rewarding relationships and other societal bonds.

But did you know empathy is now believed to have a strong genetic basis as well? Some children will forever remain locked out of common emotional experiences. Such people are known as *sociopaths*. Many high-functioning sociopaths learn how to mimic empathetic states, and some actually find their lack of empathy empowering. Some go on to become accomplished scientists, surgeons, entrepreneurs, and military commanders, professions where lack of empathy can actually be of great benefit. (Being insensitive to another individual's pain and suffering can be useful when forced to make difficult decisions concerning the fate of armies or nations.) Of course, some sociopaths take a much darker path, their empathic deficit leading them to practice anti-social behaviors, including criminal activity.

In all, about a third of all personality traits, particularly openness, conscientiousness, extraversion, agreeableness, and neuroticism, appear to be rooted in our DNA. The remaining two-thirds is strongly influenced by our environment and upbringing. So while such factors such as sexual preference, intelligence, and extroversion appear to be hereditary and immutable, more than half of our personality can be traced back to our experiences during childhood and adolescence. How our parents treated us, our relationships with our siblings, whether we were raised in wealth and privilege or poverty and neglect, how race, income, and economic opportunities affected our choices, all played a significant role in creating the people we are today.

And we certainly can't discount the impact childhood trauma can play on our developing minds. Children and teenagers who have been the victims of sexual abuse, who survived violent accidents, suffered from near-fatal illnesses, or who endured the loss of a parent or sibling due to death, abandonment, or divorce, carry with them psychological scars that impact their thoughts and behaviors for the rest of their lives. Even frequent family moves can significantly and permanently alter a child's personality.

For insights into the person you are, it can be helpful to examine the person you once *were* and the factors that impacted the course of your development. It may then become necessary to *mindbreak* to free yourself from negative attitudes and behaviors grounded in your upbringing, and *mindshift* to new, more productive, and healthier ways of thinking.

Empowering and Pernicious

Like you, I am a product of both my genetics and my upbringing. Genetically, I am full-blooded South Asian, the product of hundreds of generations who have lived on the Indian subcontinent since the first Indo-Europeans arrived around 4,000 B.C. This heritage gave me my brown complexion, dark hair, and brown eyes. From my particular family line, I also inherited a comfortably high level of both general intelligence and empathy. As for my upbringing, I can only describe it as both empowering and pernicious.

I was born in Belvidere, Illinois, a small city situated in far north-central part of the state, near the Illinois/Wisconsin border, approximately 75 miles northwest of downtown Chicago. The city's most notable feature was—and remains—its Chrysler assembly plant, which opened in the mid-1960s. During its first 10 years, it manufactured the Chrysler Newport (sedan) and Plymouth Fury (coupe), midsized cars designed and priced for the great American middle-class. Today, it produces the Jeep Cherokee. (In 2006, the plant became the first Chrysler factory with a body shop run completely via robots.) The plant was—and continues to be—so central to the Belvidere economy it's considered the city's unofficial town hall.

The city is also known for the massive F4 tornado that tore through the city on April 21, 1967, killing 24 people, many high school students who were just leaving class at the time. The disaster left a psychic scar on the city that remains to this day. At the time I was born, the city had a population of only about 15,000 (it's more than 25,000 today). Then as now, the city's residents were predominantly white, with Asians and South Asians accounting for less than one-half of 1 percent of the population. My family was, to the say the least, part of a very small and very conspicuous minority.

The eldest of three daughters, I was born to first-generation Indian-Americans. My father, Kanti, was from Anklav, a small city in Gujarat, India's western-most state. Gujarat is noted for containing several sites settled by the ancient Indus Valley Civilization, a Bronze Age people who dominated the area more than 4,000 years ago. One of these sites, the coastal city of Lothal, is believed to be one of the world's first seaports. Although Gujarat has a population of more than 60 million, Anklav itself is—and was—relatively small. Today its population is just under 20,000.

My father earned his bachelor's degree in mechanical engineering from Maharaja Sayajirao University in Vadodara, India. That August, he moved to the United States to study at Oklahoma State University in Stillwater, Oklahoma, where he earned a master's degree in industrial engineering in 1964. He used that degree to get work as an industrial engineer at RCA's assembly plant in Indianapolis, Indiana, earning the then-princely salary of $525 per month. He was subsequently offered a job at the Sundstrand Corp. in Belvidere, where I was born. Because Sundstrand was a defense contractor working on aerospace applications, my father was not recruited to the military draft during the Vietnam War.

In 1971, my father got a job as an industrial engineer at the First National Bank building in downtown Chicago. Because he was a bank employee, he was able to get a low-interest mortgage, with which he purchased a $37,000 house in Naperville, Illinois, a town about 33 miles west of downtown Chicago. At the time we moved to Naperville, the community had a population of only about 25,000. Today it's 150,000. This is where my two sisters were born.

In 1978, my father got a job working for Rockwell Collins, an aerospace company in Santa Ana, California, and moved us from suburban Chicago to Orange County. This is where most of my story takes place.

Looking back, I remember my father as being a man of great wisdom, sweetness, and kindness. Open and honest and an excellent communicator, he was a great father as well as a magnificent friend-guide-mentor-teacher guru. My mother, Vasu, was also born in Gujarat, in the village of Vasad, only a few miles east of Anklav. My mother did not receive much in terms of a formal education. She is, however, a highly intelligent woman whose wisdom comes from life experience.

She and my father had a traditional arranged marriage, one worked out by their parents. They were betrothed before he left for the United States. After earning his master's degree at Oklahoma State, he returned to Gujarat to marry her. He took her back with him to America, where they have remained ever since.

My memories of childhood are mostly positive. We were a close-knit family that assimilated quickly and eagerly into the middle-American mainstream. In fact, I have often described us as an "Indian Brady Bunch." We shared the same values, attitudes, and goals as our native-born neighbors. We believed in hard work, in obeying the rules, in the value of education, and in being responsible members of our community.

Due to the fact my parents were first-generation Indian-Americans, Indian ethics and philosophies shaped my early mind. I was raised to believe in *dharma*—that there is a "right way of living"—in *karma*—the spiritual notion of cause and effect—in *samsara*—the idea that all elements of the universe, including life itself, are cyclical—in *meditation*—the need to clear the mind of extraneous thoughts (i.e. *mindbreak*)—in *renunciation*—the need to reject harmful values and ideas (i.e., *mindshift*)—and *reincarnation*—the belief we live multiple lives until the soul is perfected.

Indian traditions also factored much into my formative years, connecting me with something bigger than myself. Holidays we enjoyed together included *Diwali*, the Festival of Lights, a five-day celebration of the victory of good over evil; *Holi,* the Festival of Colors, honoring the coming of spring; *Ganesha Chaturthi*, centered around the birth of Ganesha, son of Shiva; *Krishna Janmashtami,* a two-day-long festival celebrating the birth of Lord Krishna; and *Maha Shivratri*, a solemn holiday paying homage to Lord Shiva, and Paryushan, a Jainist holiday involving eight days of penance.

Although my family and I maintained strong ties to our Jainist religion, culture and traditions, we also adapted to many American customs, holidays, and festivals, including Independence Day, Thanksgiving, and Christmas. Growing up, I gleefully consumed American pop culture, including music, television, and movies. As a kid, my favorite TV shows included *Wonder Woman, The Electric Company*, and reruns of *Lost in Space*. I was, for all intents and purposes, an all-American girl.

This is not to say my life was as perfect as the characters I admired on TV. Not at all ...

A Double-Edged Sword

Even when I was young, my father had very high hopes for me. "You're great. You can do anything," he would often tell me. Such praise was decidedly a double-edged sword. On one hand, I always felt loved, wanted, and appreciated. I have heard people complain how their parents regularly belittled them, criticized them, and made them feel inadequate, feelings that haunted them well into adulthood. This was not my case. In fact, I was praised so highly it set a performance standard I feared I could never meet.

The fact was, as a child, I was less than perfect. Far less. For one, I was overweight. Being Indian in a basically all-white community was difficult enough, but being "chubby" undermined my self-confidence further. As a young student, I also developed a stuttering problem. Whether this had a physiological root or was a manifestation of my own insecurities, I don't know. Either way, it made my situation even worse. Finally, I was not the best student. Like the East Asians—the Chinese and Japanese—Indian-Americans have been stereotyped in America as a "model minority," people who are well-behaved, law-abiding, and superior academically, especially in math. (Today, the Indian or Pakistani computer geek is an almost universal stock character in TV shows and movies.)

But this was not the case for me. Even as young as age 6, I knew I had an academic deficit. When I was in first grade, my father gave me a puzzle designed to teach me how to tie my shoes using a simple mathematical formula. As you can imagine, being designed for a first-grader, it was pretty easy. Or at least it was supposed to be. I tried it, and quickly became confused and intimidated. The more I failed, the more nervous I became. I desperately wanted to please my father, to show him I could master such a simple task, but this desperation only made my failure that much more painful. Finally, I developed my own eclectic system of shoe-tying, a method I still use to this day.

My natural aversion to traditional academic achievement continued to haunt me throughout grammar school. I found every class to be a chore. *A painful chore.* I had to apply all the energy, concentration, and discipline I could muster just to maintain B's and C's. It quickly became apparent I was never going to be a valedictorian. My greatest ambition became to just get through each course and graduate.

Realizing I was never going to be the smartest girl in class, I decided I would try to be the nicest. To me, success was measured as a function of how many people liked me. The larger my circle of friends, the stronger my self-confidence and feelings of self-worth. To paraphrase the famous Green Bay Packers coach Vince Lombardi, to me, being liked wasn't everything, it was the *only* thing.

Looking into the future, one of my ambitions was to be a wife and mother. Having a loving family was the definition of true happiness. I practiced this maternal role with my younger sister, Arti, who is nearly 10 years my junior. As the big sister, I was also her surrogate mother, a role I eagerly embraced. I wanted to make things better for her. To watch and care for her.

My relationship with my other sister, Amy, was different. Closer in age, we saw each other as equals. In fact, I needed her as much as she needed me. It was a symbiotic relationship that continues to this day. This powerful desire to be a caretaker, to bear responsibility for other people's happiness, was a compulsion that would continue to help—and haunt—me well into adulthood.

Childhood Trauma

Earlier, I spoke of how a childhood trauma—be it major or minor—can have a long-lasting impact on someone's personality. This was, unfortunately, the case with me. When I was 10 years old, I was sexually assaulted. As it is with so many childhood victims, the perpetrator happened to be someone well known to me. A family friend. To preserve his privacy, let's call him Jed.

At the time, Jed was 25-years old. Like my parents, he was a first-generation Indian-American. Born in India, he had lived in the United States for several years. As in suburban Chicago, the Indian-American community in Orange County was, at the time, quite small, so we were a close-knit group. Virtually everyone knew everybody else, and it was not uncommon for us to spend time at each other's homes. Jed was one of the adults I met at occasional get-togethers, and he seemed friendly. I did not know at the time that he was, perhaps, a little *too* friendly.

On the evening of the incident, he and several other friends were over at our house for dinner and watching TV. Although it was a Saturday night, I went to bed at 8:30 p.m., which was my usual bedtime. A few minutes later, I heard my door open. I turned and opened my eyes, surprised to see a tall, slender male figure standing in the doorway, his silhouette backlit by the hallway light behind him. For a moment, he hesitated, then quietly slipped into my darkened bedroom, closing the door behind him.

I had no idea what was going on. I was startled, but not yet afraid. Like I said, I knew Jed. He never seemed like anything more than a "nice guy." I thought maybe he just came in to wish me goodnight. Curiously, I watched as he sat down beside me. Again, he hesitated, then ran his hand over the top of my head. I began to speak—I wanted to know what he was doing in my bedroom—but he pursed his lips and made an insistent "Shhh"-ing sound. I immediately clammed up. I didn't know what he might do next, but I was afraid if I protested or called out he might hurt me.

My body tensed as he shifted his position, raised the blankets on his side of the bed, then slowly laid himself down to face me. He stared into my eyes—which were now wide open with fright—before placing his right hand on my right arm, so I would not move. This time, his hands kept moving. Down to my chest. My stomach. My breasts.

Now I wanted to scream, but knew I dared not make a sound.

After what seemed like an eternity, he removed his hand and again traced his fingers up my body and back to my face. Right after that, he kissed me hard on the lips to my shock and abhorrence. He then laid his index finger on my lower lip, then quietly slipped out of bed. My jaw remained clenched as he returned to the door. He opened it slightly, a sliver of light lancing into my bedroom. Seeing the coast was clear, he left, closing the door behind him.

Alone again, I could breathe. Tears began to well up in my eyes and my body began to shake uncontrollably like it had when I'd gone swimming in our community pool and emerged from the water into a cool breeze. Thankfully, there had been no sexual penetration. But still I felt violated.

In the years following this incident, questions circled my mind, like why had Jed done this? Why was this my first kiss? I suspect part of his aberrant behavior can be linked to India's traditionally repressive culture. Although it produced the Kamasutra, the celebrated third century manual on love and sex, it also produced the caste system, a model of strict social stratification in which everyone "knew their place." This includes women, regardless of social standing. For centuries, India had been a predominantly agrarian country, and it was not uncommon for girls to be betrothed to future husbands even in infancy. Girls could be married off even before they achieved physical puberty. Though we have combatted old forms of thinking with awareness and education, for most of its history, India did not grant women property rights and most other civil rights. We were chattel. This is the culture Jed came from.

It took me years to realize Jed was also likely unsure of his own manhood. New to America, he was just now encountering women who were becoming "liberated"—not only empowered financially and politically, but also sexually. To a person like Jed, contemporary women represented an existential threat to his sense of masculinity. A child, on the other hand, was still weak, subservient, and compliant, the way he likely thought all women were supposed to be.

As for myself, I was very confused by the incident for a long time. At that age, I greatly admired the classic all-American cheerleader: the tall, thin, blue-eyed blonde with perfect breasts, a tiny waist, and long, well-toned legs. On TV, my role model was Wonder Woman, a woman of unrivaled intellect, physicality, and strength. In other words, I admired females who were everything I was not. Nor did I ever believe I could be. That Jed found *me* attractive left me very confused. Just 10 years old, I had already begun to develop breasts, and this had made me feel extremely self-conscious. Perhaps this development was why Jed felt himself attracted to me.

At the same time, I was repelled by Jed's behavior. I had a faint idea of what sexual assault was, and I had a pretty good idea this fit the description. So what was I supposed to do about it? Tell my parents? To be honest, I was terrified of not being believed. Of being humiliated. Or, worst of all, of being blamed. In the years that followed, I learned these were exactly the reasons most women never report sexual assault. It's just too painful an experience to be grilled about.

This single encounter plagued me for years even though I kept it to myself. As I grew into adolescence, I wished I had someone I could talk to about it without judgment. A friend. A therapist. Anybody. But, for a long time, this was a secret I felt I could trust with no one. Not even the man who became my husband. (By the way, I underwent Eye Movement Desensitizing and Reprocessing – also known as EMDR – with a psychologist to ensure I did not have any underlying issues associated with this trauma. EMDR is a relatively new form of psychotherapy often used to treat people suffering from Post-Traumatic Stress Disorder [PTSD], whose symptoms often mirror those of sexual assault.)

As evidenced by my story, we all have baggage we carry from childhood. It may not be as traumatizing as sexual assault. It may just be a series of minor humiliations or failures. Regardless of their objective importance, such traumas can shape our personalities and behaviors well into adulthood. But we need not be prisoners of our pasts. Through *mindbreaking* and *mindshifting,* we can learn to face life BRAVELY with confidence, courage, and optimism—as the following story reveals.

Case Study: Axel

Axel was a 20-year-old Indian-American male living at home while attending college. Born in the United States, he was sent to India as a toddler to live with his grandparents because his single mother could no longer take care of him. Although raised with love by his grandparents, this early separation left him with long-lasting emotional scars.

It wasn't until years later that he managed to return to the U.S. and reunite with his mother, her new husband, and his new stepsister. He found his stepfather to be strict and controlling, a situation that led to frequent fights and recriminations. His mother remained fairly neutral during these encounters, failing to provide the support he felt he needed. Numerous traumas experienced over many years in multiple locations left Axel feeling depressed, with little hope for the future.

When I first met him, Axel was living with his blended family under strict house rules. He attended a local college, pursuing a degree in business and working part-time in the service industry. His No. 1 goal was to better manage his emotions and develop a positive relationship with his stepfather.

Being BRAVE

Beliefs >>> *Benevoliefs* (King of the Jungle):

As a child, Axel was confident and optimistic. Unfortunately, years of trauma left him fearful and wary. When we began working together, he expressed interest in a career involving the protection of wild animals. However, he felt isolated, weak, and not prepared to accomplish this goal. Life in general overwhelmed him. He wanted to *mindshift* to the persona of a lion, capable of standing up for himself and being strong in the face of adversity.

Readiness (Taming the Tiger):

To *mindbreak* free of his confining attitudes, Axel needed to develop better communication techniques and response mechanisms to confront the challenges he regularly faced. I suggested the Boxing Ring Technique as a possible solution. When faced with blame, anger, or accusations triggering a defensive emotional response, he was to:

Maintain eye contact with his accuser, take three deep breaths, and remain silent, hearing the person out.

Regularly nod to show he was paying attention to what the other person was saying.

Try to resist entering to any major back-and-forth dialogue. Instead, just acknowledge what the other person was saying, and respond with short, powerful statements of support, validation, and love.

I recommended Axel try this for 30 days and report back. If he felt an urge to yell, argue, or otherwise engage in verbal combat, he was to simply turn and walk away. Such confrontations were, for all intents and purposes, a boxing ring, and either he or his opponent were likely get pummeled. But he was under no obligation to fight.

Instead, I helped him see he could use this technique to better manage his relationship with his stepfather. Rather than constantly confront this difficult man, Axel should instead let his stepfather have his say and use the opportunity to learn his stepfather's point-of-view and the reasons for his unhappiness.

Alignment (Advisors That Roar):

Alex is building a fierce emotional support team—an "A-Team"—including his mentor, a close friend, and myself. Together we are providing the support he needs to develop the personal, professional, and spiritual aspects of his life.

Vision (Map of The Jungle):

Axel wishes to *mindshift* to the persona of a brave leader, a man who takes healthy and benevolent charge of others. This vision is beginning to support and reconfigure his career map. It has also led him to bravely follow his passion: working with animals.

Engagement (Running in The Jungle):

Axel continues to have difficulty concentrating in the moment—being *mindful*—as he is regularly troubled by his difficult past. Based on our work together, he is developing strategies to manage the guilt and fear associated with his early separation from his mother. He is also working on managing his expectations, to understand and adjust his own needs as well as those of his friends and family. To deal with others collaboratively, with respect, kindness and understanding, he is using the Boxing Ring Technique to spend the time necessary to really listen to other people rather than reacting compulsively to perceived threats.

Outcomes

As noted above, Axel is now going to school, while working part-time in the food-service industry. He has a girlfriend and appears far better adjusted than when I first met him. He reports his home life is more peaceful, and he feels more confident about his ability to cope with adversity as well as what awaits him in the future.

We are still seeing each other professionally and I am coaching him on an as-needed basis. Having worked with him for four years now, I can see the growth and maturity he has gained. He is far more capable of diffusing his anger, fear, and confusion than he was when we first met. This has led him to enjoy an overall better quality of life. He is looking forward to the future and has a solid new *benevolief.* He is King of His Jungle.

What I Learned from this Client

Childhood traumas—violations of trust, innocence, and safety—are like physical injuries; even after they have healed superficially, we can often feel their pain well into adulthood. They can even lead to long-term disability. Such traumas can often manifest themselves in unexpected ways. The four most common manifestations are:

Loss of the true self

When we encounter trauma as a child, it's natural for us to believe we are to blame for our pain. Being self-centered children, we believe the trauma is *our fault.* Therefore, if we can change who and what we are, perhaps the pain will stop. This causes many trauma victims to devise new personas they believe will be more acceptable to those causing them anguish or to better cope with the adversity they're facing. Unfortunately, this inevitably leads to conflict between the false and true self for dominance.

Victimization

Trauma leads most people to naturally see themselves as victims. Victims are, by definition, weak. Helpless. They are to be pitied. The greatest challenge for a trauma sufferer is to *mindbreak* from the "victim" mode of thinking and *mindshift* to an attitude of strong and capable self-sufficiency. Acquiring such a *benevolief* can at first appear impossible, but it is critical if one is to function as a fully realized adult.

Avoidance

A core trait of trauma disorders, avoidance is a natural tendency to steer clear of triggers or reminders of the trauma. Unfortunately, avoidance also tends to weaken the will and make one take a passive approach to life. Things happen *to you,* not *because* of you. Again, recovery from trauma demands we take an active role in our own life story. Resilience is among the most important traits to nurture to thrive in life.

Hair-Triggers

A common exterior manifestation of trauma survival is the so-called "hair-trigger." We see this occurring with former soldiers experiencing PTSD. A sudden noise, like a door slam, a firecracker pop, or an automobile backfire, can cause them to snap into a fight-or-flight mode. In cases such as Axel's, we find people who immediately expect the worst from others and approach any conflict in full combat mode. To overcome this, we must learn to step back emotionally, to not take every conflict as an existential threat, and, above all, to practice empathy. By connecting with adversaries on an emotional level, we can learn to diffuse conflicts and find the basis for peace and cooperation.

Quote:

"Removing blockages from your past leaves you free to move forward and get what you want out of life."

For contemplation:

Do you have a core wound (or more than one)? How did it affect you when it happened, and how does it now? How do you nurture it? What have you done to heal it?

Affirmation:

"All of my wounds are healing themselves."

Exercise: Inner Child

I don't like to reinforce pain from the past by referencing our so-called "inner child." Rather, I let my clients know it's imperative to understand exactly where we have been and more importantly, where we are now. I remind them life is a process of continuous discovery. To release the pain of your past, I recommend you make a list of three to five self-reflective questions concerning the most disturbing part of your childhood. Afterwards, create a column filled with helpful suggestions you would give as a present adult to your former inner child. Doing so will put you into a *mindshift* thought pattern, allowing you to take back control and yet also adopt a forgiving, loving mindset.

Chapter 4
How Adolescence Taught Me Not to Be Brave

Upheaval

My childhood can be divided into two distinct parts. The first covered my first nine years spent in suburban Chicago. The second covered my childhood and adolescent years in Orange County. The move occurred in 1978 when my father left his job working as an industrial engineer for the First National Bank of Chicago to join Rockwell Collins in Santa Ana. Headquartered in Cedar Rapids, Iowa, but with plants throughout the United States, Rockwell Collins specialized in communications devices for the civilian and military aircraft industries, which fit perfectly with my father's area of expertise.

This new job represented a major career opportunity and required our family to move from Naperville 2,000 miles west to Orange County, the massive suburban sprawl situated some 50 miles southeast of Los Angeles. After looking at homes throughout Orange County, he and my mom finally settled on a two-story, four-bedroom home in what was then the fledgling city of Mission Viejo.

Although the move was necessarily traumatic for me, I also regarded with a child's sense of giddy anticipation.

As a child growing up in the Midwest, California— especially Southern California—had an aura of mystery and romance that made it almost mythic. I couldn't imagine a place more unlike where I had been born and raised. First, there was the weather. For a good six months out of the year, temperatures in the Chicago area ranged from merely unpleasantly cold to downright dangerously frigid. Beginning in mid-October, the mercury would drop to 50 degrees or lower, usually accompanied by pounding rain and bone-chilling wind. As early as November, we could wake up to find dew had frozen overnight, turning lawns to carpets of fragile icicles that crunched underfoot as we crossed them.

And then the snows would come, always beautiful before transforming the city's streets into a treacherous, sloppy mess through which my parents would struggle to navigate like overmatched players in some sadistic, no-win videogame. As temperatures continued to fall, I had to don bulky, quilted pants and jackets that made me look like the cartoon Michelin Man or a miniature Macy's Thanksgiving Day Parade balloon. (Not exactly the perfect look for a girl struggling with weight issues.)

Even then, the wind-blown cold would cut through the heavy fabric and dig deep into my bones, causing me to shiver from head to toe. Maybe my Indian genes—evolved over millennia to deal with subtropical climates—made me particularly vulnerable to the brutal Illinois winters. Sure, as I kid, I freaked out over the first snowfall, loved to build snowmen, go sledding, and have wild snowball fights. But as I grew older, I found the season to be increasingly challenging. Snow was no longer something to play in but something to shovel, to sweep, to trap my father's car. (I still have vivid memories of my sisters and I huddled in our car backseat, the engine rumbling and the heater roaring, as my father worked his way around the outside of the vehicle struggling to clear away accumulated snow just so Mom could drive us to school.)

Likewise, plunging temperatures no longer represented an excuse to bake cookies and drink hot chocolate, but was the reason we wore unflattering sweaters, bulky shoes, and ended up sweating in overheated department stores.

In Naperville, spring was always slow to arrive. When it did materialize, it lasted far too briefly, giving way to summers that were hot, humid, and oppressive. The unrelenting furnace was relieved only by thunderstorms that would tear through the area like freight trains, accompanied by tornado watches or, on more than one occasion, authentic tornado warnings. Many a summer night was spent with my family huddled in our finished basement listening to the wind-driven rains pummeling our windows as local newscasters discussed tornado watches or, more frightening still, announced official warnings of actual tornados in the area.

As for entertainment, there was not that much to excite the typical preteen in Naperville. Yes, the Fox Valley Mall opened in nearby Aurora in 1975, offering the typical array of middle-class retail anchors, generic fashion boutiques, and gaudy fast food restaurants—but otherwise the city was an island amidst a sea of corn and soybean fields. (Our house's backyard actually looked out onto a cornfield.) Neighboring Chicago, with its awesome architecture, beautiful lake front, world-class museums, and endless high-end shopping, was a good hour's drive away and rarely on my parents' destination list. The Six Flags Great America theme park, located in the city of Gurnee, was even farther away, the northern Illinois highway system requiring any Napervillian to first drive due east into Chicago before turning north and traveling another half hour toward the Illinois/Wisconsin border to get there. And, due to the area's uncooperative weather, the park was only open from mid-April through mid-October. In all, I only managed to visit the park a few times before we moved.

In short, there was little about Naperville I was going to miss. I even avoided the trauma most kids suffer when their family pulls up stakes and moves cross-country, forcing them to abandon close friends. Although I was "friendly" with several of my grammar school classmates, I wouldn't describe our relationships as particularly close. Therefore, my departure contained none of the tearful farewells and solemn promises to write daily so popular in teen fiction. I expected I would quickly forget them and they would quickly forget me.

The Golden State

Any trepidation I might have held about the move was overwhelmed by my excitement over moving to Southern California. Like most Midwestern kids, I harbored a romantic image based on years of exposure to movies and TV shows set in La-La Land. In my tender young brain, Southern California meant sunny beaches, tanned surfers, glamorous movie stars, sprawling mansions, the L.A. Dodgers, towering palm trees, and Brady Bunch-style suburbs.

Best of all, there was no winter. This last notion was not a whimsical fantasy but irrefutable fact. I had witnessed this miracle myself on multiple occasions as I watched the annual Tournament of Roses parade play out on my family's 27-inch Zenith TV. While snow drifted outside our living room window and glistening icicles formed along the edge of our roof, here before me stood thousands of smiling, sun-drenched parade-goers dressed in nothing but jeans and short-sleeved shirts, the off-screen announcers describing sunny skies and temperatures in the low 70s. How I longed to be part of that jubilant throng!

Had we moved in January or February, the accompanying temperature shock would have no doubt been extremely dramatic. But we didn't leave until late June as my parents wanted my sisters and me to first complete our school term. After sending all of our earthly possessions ahead through Mayflower Movers, we were all flown from Chicago to Orange County Airport courtesy of my father's new employer.

From the airport, we drove down the I-405 freeway into Mission Viejo in the heart of what locals called "South County." As I later learned, Mission Viejo ("Green Mission" in Spanish, and named for an ancient Spanish land grant) was one of the last parts of Orange County to be developed.

The area is very hilly and was for decades avoided by residential and commercial builders who felt the local geography was just too daunting to make development profitable. So it was used for cattle grazing until the late 1960s when developer Donald Bren, who later became chairman and owner of the powerful Irvine Company, presented a plan for a massive community built around a 125-acre artificial lake. Once the county approved the proposal in the early 1970s, the City of Mission Viejo sprang into existence, becoming one of the largest master-planned communities in the United States. (Today it is second only to Highlands Ranch, Colorado, south of Denver, in terms of size).

Acclimation

Several things struck me upon our arrival, signaling to me we "weren't in Kansas anymore." (And certainly not in Illinois.) The first was topography. As I noted earlier, northern Illinois, like most of the Midwest, is pretty flat. We had a few low rolling hills, dips, and ravines here and there, but when it came to actual elevation, the highest you were ever likely to travel was across a freeway overpass. By contrast, Mission Viejo is all hills. Located on the northeast side of the Saddleback Valley (after Saddleback Mountain, the county's highest mountain, elevation 5,689 feet, part of the Santa Ana mountain range), Mission Viejo consists of dozens of hillside neighborhoods connected by broad, four- and six-lane roads rising and falling and twisting and turning like some city-sized amusement park ride.

And then there was the architecture. Back in Naperville, buildings comprised a mix of old and new with some older homes dating back to the 19th century. Homes in Naperville represented a broad mix of styles from traditional Cape Cod, craftsman, Colonial, ranch, Tudor, Victorian, and what I can only describe as "post-war brick bungalow." In Mission Viejo, practically every building was brand new, and almost every house was built in the same Spanish Mission style with stucco walls and barrel-tile roofs.

As I later learned, the stucco, which covers flexible wooden frames, made these homes resistant to the minor earthquakes that regularly rumbled through the area, whereas bricks would easily crack, crumble, and even collapse during such temblors. ("Temblor" is another word I had to learn as a newly minted Californian. Like so many transplants, I originally pronounced the word as "trembler," only to be quickly corrected.) And while virtually every house in Naperville had a basement that could serve as a tornado shelter, here such subterranean refuges were non-existent. All homes were built on simple concrete slabs. When there are no tornados, why bother building a basement?

The More Things Change, the More They Stay the Same

But while Mission Viejo and Naperville were wildly different on the surface, they shared many important characteristics that would continue to shape my life. For one, like the city from which I had just escaped, Mission Viejo was—and continues to be—prominently Caucasian. Almost blindingly so. Although the city has, in the ensuing years, become somewhat diverse (in the 2010 census, the city's population was still 80 percent white), when I began sixth grade that fall, I was the only Indian-American on the student roster. Even when I got to high school four years later, there were only a few Indian-Americans in the entire school.

Needless to say, for years I was the odd-girl out. I looked different. I talked differently. I had different points of reference. I liked deep dish pizza and didn't know what an animal style In-N-Out Burger was. I didn't surf or skateboard—heck, at first, I didn't even own a swimsuit—and wore gloves when the temperature dipped below 55. My parents drove an American car, not a Japanese or German import. As a result of these and countless other cultural incongruities, whenever I would go out with other students—to the beach, on dates, or just hang out at the Mission Viejo mall—I always questioned my place. I never felt like I fit in. Because of the constant pressure to conform, I felt like I could never be my authentic self.

All through my adolescence, all I ever wanted was to be respected for who and what I was. But it was not to be. As a young teenager, I had only one truly close friend. Her name was Amisha. I met her through my younger sister. Like me, she was Indian-American, born in India but brought to the U.S. as a toddler, so she had no personal memories of her home country.

I suspect much of our initial bonding was due to our shared status as ethnic soulmates. At a time when South Asians—both Indians and Pakistanis—were not nearly as common in Orange County as they are today—and with emotionally stunted adolescents eager to sort each other into cliques based on race, family income status, collegiate ambitions, extracurricular interests, athletic ability, fashion sense, music tastes, and even type of car driven— we naturally gravitated to each other for validation and support. Her presence was, to me, a gift, one I continue to cherish to this day.

Like the stereotypical high school popularized in movies from the '80s like *Fast Times At Ridgemont High* and *The Breakfast Club,* our student body was self-segregated into jocks, cheerleaders, popular kids, mean girls, surfers, science nerds, computer dorks, videogame addicts, theater geeks, stoners, troublemakers, wannabes, and foreigners. Although Amisha and I were technically as American as apple pie, in a sea of European white, our skin color and unusual surnames consigned us to one of the outlier categories. Fortunately, our compatibility went far beyond mere melanin, as we shared many interests, likes, dislikes, and tastes. We quickly became inseparable becoming BFFs (even though the term had yet to be coined), and forged a relationship that remains strong and vital to this day.

New Locale, Old Patterns

The move from Naperville to Mission Viejo may have provided me with the proverbial fresh start socially, but it did nothing to improve my scholastics. I continued to be an average student, earning an inalterable string of B's and C's, along with as the occasional A. While my classmates prepared for careers as lawyers, doctors, entrepreneurs, financiers, software developers, and even Hollywood screenwriters, I naively entertained fantasies of going into fashion design or even (gasp) news anchoring. Never mind that my artistic abilities were sub-nominal, my fashion sense was largely dictated by fashion retailers and 1980s music videos, or that my looks, voice, and stutter made a career in news anchoring about as likely as me winning a Nobel Prize in physics, I was still young enough to dream.

Pragmatists through and through, my parents did not share my lofty ambitions. Being traditional, conservative Indians, they wanted me to pursue a career in either medicine, science, or business. (Or at least go to a college where I was likely to meet and marry a future doctor, scientist, or businessman.) But again, such a classically bourgeois scenario was just not in the cards, and I knew it. Although Indians have been recognized as being one of the most affluent ethnic group in America, all bell curves have outliers and, even as a teen, I could tell I was destined to occupy a data point well on the end of the spectrum.

By the time I was 15, my parents finally resigned themselves to the fact academics were never going to be my strong suit. Thus, they subtly altered their strategy. If I wasn't going to be the next poster child for Indian-American overachievement, I would at least meet a "nice

Indian boy" with whom I could eventually settle down and produce a litter of nice Indian babies.

To this end, they encouraged me to attend as many Indian clubs, festivals, and cultural events as they could find within easy driving distance of our home. As it turned out, the city of Cerritos, which happened to be situated just a 30-minute drive to the north, had a large Indian-American population and staged an Indian cultural dance festival every year.

Young Love

The cultural festival featured *garba*, a form of dance that originated in my parents' home state of Gujarat. Traditionally performed during the nine-day Hindu festival of *Navaratri*, garba is a circular dance performed around a centrally lit lamp or a picture or statue of the Goddess Durga.

It was at this garba dance festival that I met Umesh. I was still 15 and he was 19. The fact that this "older man" took an interest in me made him instantly attractive to me, and we crushed on each other fast and hard. What made Umesh particularly appealing was that he was an Indian "bad boy."

Rebellious in both his wardrobe and behavior, he wore jeans, not slacks. He donned trendy '80s ankle boots, not shoes. He had a brazen, nonconformist attitude that made one wonder what he would do next. He was, in short, the antithesis of the kind of mature, respectful, and career-oriented young man my parents wanted me to date. Which is probably exactly why I was eager to date him.

And date we did. Often we'd just hang out with his friends, party, and make out. In all, we dated for about two years. And, believe it or not, we never had sex. We did practically everything else but, even as a high school junior, I just wasn't ready to "go all the way," and Umesh didn't pressure me. At not least strongly.

Predictably, my earlier sexual assault made me skittish whenever the possibility of sex presented itself. He seemed to get the signal, because it never went much further. In spite of not consummating our relationship—it was still a very special one for both of us—what happened next really hurt.

Between my junior and senior years in high school, my wild teenage romance came to a sudden, painful end. I was in my bedroom getting ready to go out when Umesh called to say he was moving to Atlanta. A relative had secured a job for him there and he had agreed to take it.

Why Umesh chose to tell me this over the phone rather than in person was a question I only began to ponder later. I can only imagine he was simply too embarrassed—or nervous—to break up face-to-face. Even at age 21, Umesh was still very much a teenager, concerned foremost about his personal needs and not the young girl he had been romancing for the past 24 months.

The next day, Umesh came by my house to say his final goodbye. He had already packed his things and was preparing to make the cross-country drive to Georgia in the same used car in which he'd taken me out. Our awkward parting lasted about an hour. We promised to stay in touch, to phone when we could, and write each other regularly. Our last kiss was long, hard, and tinged with the salt of my tears.

As I watched him drive away, I felt like someone had punched me in the chest. Right over my heart. The rational side of my mind had long known our relationship couldn't last forever, that we'd eventually drift apart and that our time together would become just the kind of pleasant memory characters talked about in the movies. But that day, with the taste of Umesh's kiss still on my lips, the pain was real and immediate and I couldn't believe I would ever recover.

Endings and Beginnings

The heartbreak over the loss of my first romance lasted a long time. During my whole senior year of high school, I didn't have a boyfriend and didn't date. My breakup with Umesh had left me in an emotional black hole from which I could not escape without another dramatic and jarring change of scene.

This change occurred in the fall. Despite my less-than-stellar academic performance, I managed to be admitted to the University of Southern California's Marshall School of Business. There, I resolved to earn a bachelor's degree in marketing. By this time, I had abandoned my news anchoring ambitions as well as any hope of becoming a professional fashion designer. Still, I figured that with a marketing degree, I might still have a chance of getting into the fashion world on the business side.

My years at 'SC (as we liked to call it) were, socially, one of the best experiences I have ever had. I reveled in the independence. The growth opportunities. The chance to connect with people from all over the world. At the same time, I continued to struggle scholastically. I faced each test with the same level of dread most people reserve for visiting the dentist.

Fortunately, by this time, any delusions my parents clung to about my academic prowess had also evaporated. They no longer pressured me to succeed as they had when I lived with them. In fact, in my junior year, when I told my father I was failing Business Law, he said something to me I never thought I'd ever hear pass his lips: "It's okay to get a C. The point is to graduate. To get your diploma. When you go into the working world, no one is going to ask for your report card or your GPA."

This parental absolution provided me with enormous relief. *I could breathe.* More importantly, I finally understood perfection was not necessary for success. Or happiness. Years later, I would read a quote from filmmaker and comedian Woody Allen who said, "Eighty percent of success is just showing up." My life's experience offers testament to this truth. Trying to be perfect only sets you up for failure and is an impossible standard to achieve. More often than not, just doing the work, as imperfect as it may be, is more than sufficient. And it sure makes it easier to get one's self up in the morning.

Knowing this to be true as an adult far removed from college, high school, or many of the travails young people must face navigating their way through life, I would like to now offer a case study demonstrating the importance of showing up and doing the work. Sometimes, true bravery means simply holding space—refusing to succumb to fear or the unrealistic expectations of others.

Case Study: Krish

Krish is a 20-year-old male I met during his senior year at the University of California-Irvine (UCI). Immediately, I sensed similarities between us. Though Krish was studying engineering, he had little interest in the technical career his parents had mapped out for him. Instead, he wanted to pursue an international business role with a nonprofit organization while using his artistic side to support a company whose mission he believed in.

State of Mind

This conflict between his ambitions and those of his parents had left Krish angry and confused. He wanted to follow his bliss, but at the same time did not want to disappoint his mother and father. He wanted his family to be proud of him but didn't believe they would support his aspirations.

Situation

Krish came to me in the hopes we could develop a series of talking points he could present to his parents to explain his professional choices through respectful and mature communication. At the same time, he wanted help identifying specific steps he could take to secure his dream job.

Status

Accomplishing his goals required Krish to gain a level of courage he had not yet experienced. He would have to *mindbreak* free of the passive, obedient attitude he had held for most of his life and *mindshift* to something bolder, braver, and more self-assured. The road ahead was unknown. Rejection on both fronts was a clear possibility. Only by strengthening his self-confidence and resolve could he possibly achieve his desired goals.

Beliefs >>> *Benevoliefs* (Self-Mastery)

Krish originally believed he was forever beholden to his parents. To honor them, he felt he must live his life according to their desires and dictates. His *mindshift* would take him to a place where he was master of his own fate. He could go beyond his parents' college game plan and take the risks necessary to achieve a different outcome.

Readiness (Road Map Needed)

It was not enough for Krish to simply resolve to take action. He had to create a series of well-considered steps and devise a specific schedule by which he could execute his job search. Then he had to find the discipline to execute his plan, staying focused while tamping down his inner, inhibiting voice holding him back through guilt and negativity.

Alignment (Summoning a Tribe)

Krish was able to assemble a powerful team of allies. In addition to my input, he garnered support from his college friends and helpful contacts within the nonprofit community. These people not only provided him with encouragement, but also specific advice on how to find employment opportunities, whom to contact, how to construct his resume, and how to present himself in interviews.

Vision (Following the Trail)

Krish's vision of a satisfying job in the nonprofit industry kept him firmly on his path to success. Day by day, he adhered to this vision until, six months later, he was offered the position he so passionately desired. Through this experience, he learned the importance of having a road map—a strategic plan. He now knows that regardless of his objective, *planning* is half the battle.

Engagement (Running Free)

Once Krish learned to manage his fears, he was able to graduate and then sit down with his parents to explain his plan to secure a non-engineering position. Much to his relief, the encounter went well and, a few months later, he left the United States to become a project manager with a nonprofit organization in his ancestral land of India.

I was able to connect with Krish through both our shared ethnic ancestry and our similar paternal relationships. We both had parents who set high expectations for us, which caused us distress when we failed to live up to their lofty standards. We both had to learn to understand and respect where our parents were coming from, while at the same time charting our own paths and learning to find our own ways in the world.

Through our sessions together, Krish and I made a career search plan to pursue his new personal and professional interests, implementing strategic communication, strengthening his focus, and creating a disciplined schedule of related actions and personal risk management. The plan included a detailed step-by-step daily regimen, including stress-management exercises using meditation and visualization, dedicated time spent on creative networking and messaging, and sending resumes on a preset schedule. Every activity was monitored and recorded. We were careful to create a series of metrics by which he could measure his level of success over time.

Quote:

"It's not how high the mountain is, it's your perception of it."

For contemplation:

Have you ever felt out of place? When and why? Do you still?

Affirmation:

I establish and live up to my own expectations.

Exercise:

Close your eyes and visualize taking a hike on a mountain. At the points where you push yourself because the terrain is a little more challenging, notice how you must alter your breathing and strengthen your mental resolve. Then reach for the tools you need, such as your hiking poles, water, or music. Confirm this imagined experience by writing down what you are feeling with your mind and body.

Keep yourself focused on the goal you set to move through the uncomfortable part of your imagined journey. At the end, write down what you experienced during the trek and the celebratory emotions you felt when completed. Remember, you only feel out of place, restless, and uncomfortable when you are not prepared for new and challenging environments. This is an example of a visualization technique where you partner with your mindset to transform your perspective and eventually the outcome.

Chapter 5
How My Marriage Taught Me Not to be Brave

Like many people, I tend to measure life's progress as a function of my romantic relationships. My high school years were all about finding love, and Umesh was a large part of that. He was my first love, and it was through him that I experienced my first feelings of romantic longing, sexual excitement and, ultimately, heartbreak. College, on the other hand, was all about meeting educational goals and having a variety of dating experiences. By the time I neared my 20th year, the pain from my breakup with Umesh had faded to a dull ache and I was ready to accept the attention—and affections—of another male.

I met my next boyfriend around the time of my college graduation. Kent was the perfect candidate. *The anti-Umesh.* Whereas Umesh was Indian-American, Kent was 100 percent WASP. Whereas Umesh was dark-haired and had a medium-tan skin tone, Kent was blond and white. While Umesh was very attractive, his looks were decidedly unconventional, yet Bollywood level in my eyes. Kent, on the other hand, had the classic, symmetrical looks of a fashion model or movie star. In fact, one particular movie star. Think a young Robert Redford—the smooth-skinned, killer-grin *Barefoot in the Park* and *Butch Cassidy and the Sundance Kid* Robert Redford.

Kent and I dated for three years. Despite the differences in our cultures and upbringing—or perhaps because of them—we clicked like characters in some fluffy romantic comedy. He found me exotic and I found validation in a guy whose looks, confidence, and charisma qualified him to be cast as the star quarterback, student council president, or a U.S. senator-in-the-making. Happily, it turned out we had plenty in common, including a love of Mexican and Italian food, Nirvana, Red Hot Chili Peppers, liberal politics, surfing, (he surfed, I watched), and visiting his grandparents, his favorite people in the world.

More than anything, Kent imbued me with a sense of confidence I had never felt before. I felt so strong with him that I finally found the courage to accept him as my first sexual partner. Awkward at first, our sex quickly became an exciting and, for me, wholly new dimension of our relationship. I was not the first girl he'd had sex with, and I was grateful to be the recipient of his experience. He was gentle and attentive. He never made me feel embarrassed or silly. He made me appreciate my body and wanted to please me, which of course, made me eager to please him too.

Considering My Options

By the end of our third year together, Kent and I were looking ahead to achieving our professional goals in life beyond college. He was hoping to start a career as a professor, and I was, well, I was still "considering my options." Which meant I wasn't yet sure *what* I wanted to do. I only knew there was still zero chance of becoming the doctor, lawyer, or engineer my parents had fantasized about. My focus was on business, marketing, and entrepreneurship, and while my USC education provided a fantastic foundation, I didn't yet know which specific career I wanted to pursue.

In any case, our conversions about life after college always circled back to feelings about our relationship. Was this going to lead to more? I had often heard that women went to college to get their "M.R.S." degree, and it only made sense that Kent and I would get married.

Would my parents approve?

I was sure there would be some initial resistance. After all, their dream had been for me to marry a "nice Indian boy," and this blond Adonis checked none of their cultural boxes. But he was a college graduate. He came from a good, solid family. (Kent's father was a high-level finance executive for a major Southern California company.) There were no major issues in his background. No arrests. He didn't have any tattoos. And he cleaned up really nicely. All and all, he was a "good catch." The person I was meant to settle down with.

Or, so I thought.

A Blast from the Past

As it turns out, I might have gone on to become Mrs. Kent had I not gotten an unexpected phone call at 9 p.m. one fateful Thursday night. I was now living with two roommates—one of whom was Amisha—and working in Los Angeles for a large environmental company in sales. We were all sitting in the living room watching TV when the phone rang. It was Umesh calling from Atlanta. My mind rapidly did the math. Nine p.m. here on the West Coast meant it was midnight in Georgia. Anyone who calls at midnight is either conveying news of a recent death or is drunk. Umesh was not likely calling to tell me someone had died.

No, he was calling to say he was getting a divorce. *A divorce?* I was stunned. After all, I had heard he had married, but we had not been in touch after that. For the next hour, Umesh told me how, after 18 months as husband and wife, he and his wife had drifted apart. They no longer saw "eye to eye" on anything, so she had left him and gotten back with an ex-boyfriend. Umesh was devastated. Fortunately, the two never had any children, so the break would be clean and simple.

Immediately, old feelings rushed to the surface, and I started fantasizing about Umesh returning to SoCal or something along those lines. But then he said something that shocked me.

"I never stopped loving you."

"You didn't?"

"No. Even after moving to the other side of the country. Even after marrying someone else—my feelings for you never changed."

This declaration literally took my breath away. It made me examine my own feelings, and I was stunned and confused by what I discovered. Although I had been with Kent for three years, had become intimate lovers, and even contemplated a future as husband and wife, I still felt a strong, perhaps even *irresistible* longing to be with Umesh. This made no sense to me. Kent loved me and Umesh represented nothing but heartbreak. Kent was stable and dependable. Umesh, well...he wasn't exactly a rock of stability. But like so many pleasures we know are bad for us, Umesh was a temptation I simply could not resist.

A (Kind of) Clean Break

After that night, Umesh and I continued to call each other every few days. I realized that calls, no matter how frequent, would never be enough. So I asked Kent to meet me at his apartment. Wanting to be open and transparent, even if it caused us both discomfort, I told Kent everything Umesh told me, including that he still loved me.

And that I still loved him.

When I was done, I was surprised—and relieved—when Kent revealed that he knew I still had feelings for Umesh. Even so, he was understandably upset, and he tried to persuade me that I was making a mistake. After a few hours of painful and heart-wrenching discussions, I left Kent's apartment feeling shaken and guilty. I can only imagine how hurt he felt. And I didn't blame him one bit.

In retrospect, I can't imagine a more awkward, ill-planned attempt at "being honest." With another 20 years of maturity under my belt, perhaps I could have handled things better. Perhaps. Still, I was glad I had told Kent the truth. Even from the perspective of two decades, I can't imagine a scenario in which I tell my boyfriend of three years—the man I seriously intended to marry—that I'd suddenly had a change of heart and wanted to get back with my crazy high school love. No matter how mature, sensitive and empathetic I could have made the announcement, I can't see it ending any differently than it had. This was a scenario with only one possible outcome. And it was very, very painful.

Kent called me a few days later and asked to meet me for dinner. He said he wanted to talk. I gave him a very soft "no." After that, I never spoke to Kent again. Since we hadn't lived together, there was none of the awkward *"I'm coming over to get my things"* scenes common in premarital breakups. It was the kind of classic "clean break" so many relationship experts advise. One day we were a couple, the next day we weren't. And thus, another chapter in my life closed...and another began.

Umesh Redux

After I broke up with Kent, I called Umesh and offered to fly to Atlanta so we could meet face to face and determine if our renewed feelings were genuine.

He agreed.

Our reunion was almost as awkward as my breakup with Kent had been. Although we had spent years together, Umesh and I were now very different people with a vast new array of experiences behind us. In a way, we were almost strangers.

We spent a weekend together and did a lot of talking. By Sunday evening, we decided we wanted to take our relationship to the next level. Under normal circumstances, I would have said we should take things slowly. But these were not normal circumstances. We were living 3,000 miles from each other. My parents were constantly pressuring me to "get serious" with *somebody*. And I knew I wasn't getting any younger.

So Umesh began making regular weekend visits. He'd come to the apartment I was sharing with my two roommates, then we would spend time together visiting L.A.'s numerous clubs, restaurants, and friends. Each encounter was brief but oh-so intense. It turns out the sages were right: Absence had indeed made my heart grow fonder.

After several visits, we arranged for our parents to meet for the first time. And then, a mere four months after that fateful 9 p.m. phone call, we got engaged. Like everything else about Umesh, his proposal was anything but conventional. My years of watching Hollywood rom-coms had set me up for some kind of grand gesture, a ring hidden-in-the-chocolate-cake move at an ultra-fancy restaurant, or 100 red roses waiting for me when I arrived home from work, or at least him bending down on one knee while six of his friends sang "Unchained Melody" in perfect harmony. Instead, we were on the phone and he asked me, "So, what do you think? You want to get married?"

The proposal was pure Umesh: blunt. To-the-point. I answered in the only way I knew how: "Why? Do you?

This led us into a discussion of life plans, ambitions, dreams, fears, and fantasies that lasted well past midnight. Now, all that was left was for me to do was tell my parents (gulp). In the end, we agreed to tie the knot.

Breaking the (Kind of) Happy News

The next weekend, I returned to Mission Viejo to give my parents the "happy news." They might have reacted better had I announced I was dropping out of school and becoming a professional gambler. Back when I was in high school, they had disapproved of Umesh's rebel persona and his party-boy sensibilities. Now, you could add the fact that he was divorced to the list of attributes my parents deemed objectionable.

I guess I was lucky. After we made our announcement, my parents only refused to speak to me for a week after arguing. It could have been worse. Instead, they grudgingly came around to accepting Umesh as their son-in-law. I guess they figured I was mature enough to make my own decisions—and seeing me married was something we all wanted.

To their credit, my mother and father generously agreed to host our wedding: a large, traditional "Indian family style" reception at a rental hall in Buena Park, near Knott's Berry Farm. It turned out beautifully. We hosted about 200 guests with a sumptuous dinner, live music, and lively dancing lasting late into the night.

That evening, I was in heaven. Umesh and I couldn't have been happier. We had found each other again. We were in love. And true to my childhood fantasies, I felt like a princess. I felt special. Loved. Honored. Celebrated.

Everything was working out. So far ...

Hello, Houston

Late that summer, Umesh and I—now husband and wife—pulled up stakes and moved to Houston, Texas. He had family involved in oil and gas consulting in this huge port city, and they were more than happy to set Umesh up working in their company as an IT analyst. After pounding the pavement for a few months, I found work with the branch of a nationwide executive recruiting company. Now we both were getting steady paychecks! On top of that, we were young and healthy. Life was good.

Even though we were far from home, it seemed as if things were looking up. Earlier, I mentioned that the time I'd spent separated from Umesh had only intensified my feelings for him. Absence also seemed to work in Umesh's favor where my father was concerned. During those two years we spent in Texas, Umesh and my dad would frequently speak over the phone.

Somehow, unbelievably, the two began warming up to each other very, very, fast, and eventually grew to be quite fond of one another. Though separated by 1,500 miles, they bonded. Maybe it was because my dad saw Umesh was treating his eldest daughter well. Whatever the reason, my father began to accept and even love my new husband. In return, Umesh started to admire my father. Soon enough, he began seeking my dad out for guidance and advice. My dad became his surrogate parental figure. To my disbelief, they established a true connection I would have never thought possible. We all were grateful about it. And I thought it was wonderful.

Cooling Down

At the same time my father was warming up to my husband, my relationship with Umesh was becoming increasingly chilly. It's been said that the qualities that initially attract you to someone can, over time, become the sources of revulsion. At first, I had loved Umesh for his free spirit, his dismissal of authority, and for his unfettered love of life. But after five years or so of marriage, I found him to be irresponsible, undependable, and more interested in himself than in "us."

As a free spirit, he was never without the company of friends, and I noticed a marked increase in his drinking after work, on weekends, and yes, even on weekdays, too. Once he had a few drinks in his system, what few inhibitions he had evaporated. He became everybody's best friend, buying drinks for anyone within earshot. It was nice to see him so effusive and smiley, but also difficult not to be frustrated by how much money he was spending.

Night after night he would go out and drop cash with like-minded friends. Such generosity made him very popular, but it often left us with way too little money at the end of each month.

"Don't worry about money. Life is to be enjoyed!" he'd tell me when I would confront him about this problem. Meanwhile, we increasingly borrowed from Visa to pay MasterCard. And whenever I tried to reason with him about his free-spending ways, he'd call me a "party-pooper" and accuse me of dampening his fun. Finally, tired of my nagging, he'd simply leave home on his own to hang with his buddies. It wasn't long before I began to suspect that he might have a problem.

Right Back Where I Started

Two years before the turn of the millennium, Umesh and I realized Houston was no longer the place for us and decided to move back to Orange County. We found an apartment in Huntington Beach, about 20 miles northwest of our old homestead. Unlike the landlocked Mission Viejo where I had grown up, HB—commonly known as Surf City—was the poster city for beachside living.

At the time boasting a population just south of 200,000, Huntington Beach was incorporated in 1909, making it one of the oldest cities in Orange County. It was originally the site of a major oil field. Now, nearly 100 years later, local reserves had all but vanished, shifting the economy from extraction to tourism. Relatively flat and featureless compared with hilly Mission Viejo, HB is locally famous for its 9.5 miles of sandy beach, excellent surfing, and historic pier. The city is home to hundreds of rental apartment buildings and offers easy freeway access to the area's top centers of employment, including Santa Ana, Irvine, Costa Mesa, and Newport Beach. The fact that our old friends and family still lived just 15 minutes down the I-405 made our re-entry easier still.

In terms of finding work, our timing couldn't be better. It was 1998, and widespread fears over the dreaded Y2K bug had all but guaranteed a job for anyone who knew anything about computers. Not wanting to tempt fate, nearly every company, agency, and institution in the world with a mainframe went into a panic and began hiring anyone they could find who understood binary computer languages to fix or patch the Y2K bug. Umesh, who had three years of IT experience under his belt, quickly found work with a top tier IT consulting company in El Segundo and spent the next two years working to keep civilization as we knew it from collapsing.

As for me, I was able to transfer within the same executive recruitment company I had worked for in Houston to its office in Irvine, a 20-minute drive south. Within a year, I leveraged my experience to land a position with a high-tech boutique firm in Huntington Beach closer to home. Once again, Umesh and I were both gainfully employed. Within a year Umesh recruited me to join his firm, and I embarked on my first corporate HR environment. I remain grateful to him for giving me this opportunity.

Things should have been looking for up for us, especially with a big development around the corner. But life had different plans.

Happy News/Terrible News

Experts will tell you the key to a happy, successful life is to accomplish your early goals in a specific order. First, you graduate school. Then you get married. Then you have children. It seems simple, right? But an amazing number of people—especially those of the so-called X and millennial generations—do these steps out of order. Many have children before they get married. Or they marry before they finish school. Or they get married and have kids and only *then* finish school. Any one of these choices is supposed to vastly increase the chances of marital and professional difficulties.

Well, no matter how many problems were lurking on the home front, especially regarding Umesh's drinking, we had nonetheless stuck to the program. First school. Then jobs. And then marriage. The only thing left to do now was start a family. About a year after returning to Orange County, I discovered I was pregnant.

At first, Umesh and I were ecstatically happy. We had been planning to start a family soon, and this development only accelerated our pace along the path we were traveling. Feeling a sudden rush of paternal responsibility, Umesh curtailed his going out, choosing instead to nest with me. Unfortunately, our joy was short-lived. Not long after sharing the great news with my family, I received the worst phone call of my life.

My father had just passed away.

I couldn't bear or believe it. My father was everything to me. And at only 57 years old, he had so much more living to do. Besides that, he seemed strong and vital. He had had no known medical conditions. His heart was strong. His liver and kidneys were functioning perfectly. He was taking medication to control his cholesterol, but otherwise he was in perfect health. *What could have possibly gone wrong?*

Following the autopsy, we learned my father had died of a brain aneurysm. Apparently, the walls in one of his main arteries had thinned to point it could no longer stand the internal pressure. The doctor regretfully informed us aneurysms of this type can show no early symptoms and are virtually impossible to detect. If I could take any comfort in the situation, it was that except for experiencing a sudden headache, my father was probably unaware what was happening and died within hours of the aneurysm's onset.

Even though I knew Umesh and my father had grown closer in recent years, I was still surprised to see just how much my father's passing affected him. It was as if Umesh had lost his father and best friend. His feelings of anger, abandonment, and hopelessness manifested first in long stretches of silent brooding, followed by binges of alcohol consumption that could last for days.

Six months pregnant at the time, I took my father's death equally hard. To me, Dad had always represented a pillar of strength and dependability. His loss left me feeling angry, afraid, confused, and frightened. I did not see how I could navigate the perils of adulthood without his wisdom and guidance, especially since we had a baby coming.

Although my mother was still alive, I felt like my father's passing had left me alone in the world. The pain was so great it took me years to get to the point I could speak about him without my eyes welling with tears. And as much as I mourned my own loss, I felt particular grief over the fact the man I loved so very much would never meet his coming grandchild.

Welcome Sanam

Our little girl entered this world on December 3, 2000. We named her Sanam, which means "beloved." Looking back, years later, I still count this as one of the happiest days of my life. There is something special about bringing forth a child that is incomparable to any of life's other experiences. It's not just the fact that you've created this new person. It's so much more than that.

Having a child literally connects you to the past in the most fundamental of ways. Every piece of this perfect child—every strand of her DNA—came from hundreds, even thousands of ancestors going back to India and perhaps even beyond. She carries with her the entire history and heritage of our people. She also carries in her a large piece of me. Fifty percent, in fact. As such, she will transmit a piece of me into the future and, through her children, into centuries beyond. Long after I am gone, some part of me is now guaranteed to still exist. I suppose it is the closest any of us can come to achieving immortality.

I stayed at home with Sanam for 12 weeks, the longest maternity leave our company allowed. Recognizing the need to provide everything I could for my new daughter, I had already landed a position in HR recruitment for Hewlett-Packard's office in the city of Orange. Umesh's mom, my mother-in-law, volunteered to watch Sanam while I was at work, for which I remain eternally grateful. It's no exaggeration to say I missed my baby every minute I was away and couldn't wait to return home to see her. (I have to believe Umesh felt the same way.) But as time passed and we fell into our new routines, I was able to put more and more focus on my career. And this effort quickly paid off.

My First Entry to Life Coaching

After a few months, I was promoted to a Talent Team lead, responsible for taking new company hires and molding them into top-performing HP team members. In time, I learned good talent managers are essentially life coaches. We identify where our clients are strongest, where they're weakest, and point them to activities in which their talents, skills, and natural proclivities will yield the best results. Also important is learning what each employee/client wishes to achieve—what their goals are, both personally and professionally—so their individual desires and the company's objectives sync up.

Of course, being new at this, I sometimes got in over my head. I tended to overpromise to clients who wanted to achieve much but invest little effort. As a result, I had to make plans on the fly. I ended up working long hours, while balancing motherhood. Out of necessity, I learned how to deal with unpredictability and instability. Still, no matter how much I tried, in the back of my mind, I was prepared for failure.

At the same time I was working myself into a frenzy, moving into an even higher corporate role, Umesh's behavior worsened. While I was working at the office and his mother was taking care of Sanam, he was off partying with friends after work. It wasn't long before I could barely recognize the sweet man who once told me he never stopped thinking about me.

In the years since that 9 p.m. phone call, his attitude toward me had hardened. When we did see each other, his demeanor was remote and distant. He refused to talk about what he was doing or about his feelings. More and more, I felt him slipping away. Once, I learned he had spent $3,500 on a Rolex watch for a friend without discussing it as we normally would do. Such generosity might have made sense if we were killing it as a power couple bringing in millions a year, but we weren't. Money was very tight, and this kind of compulsive behavior could not be excused. The ensuing fights just left us bitter and resentful.

Some months later, Umesh left to go on what he described as a "business trip." The next day, when I did not hear from him, I called his cell phone, but only got a recorded message. This went on for several days in a row, making me increasingly worried. His mother, Sarla, who rarely showed signs of temper or distress, also became painfully worried about her son's fate. There were no emails. No texts. As far as we could tell, Umesh, Sarla's son and the father of our child, had disappeared.

*****

Before I pick up what happened to Umesh in the next chapter, I wish to tell you about a case study about one of my clients that relates to the many troubles I experienced throughout my marriage. It's my hope that Maddox's struggle and ultimate triumph over fear will inspire you to better face similar challenges in your own life.

Case Study: Maddox

When I met Maddox he was a 48-year-old white male working in sales. Although now well into middle age, he felt he still had little control over either his personal or professional life. With only a limited number of productive years left, he feared he would never live up to his true potential. Worse, he had begun resenting his wife for what he viewed as her tendency to hold him back from greatness.

Beliefs >>> *Benevoliefs* (Man of the House):

Maddox wanted to be a good provider who kept his family secure, financially and otherwise. Yet, he also felt compelled to change careers and move out of sales (which he never really enjoyed) into entrepreneurship. However, he was afraid to leave his relatively secure job and take the financial risk necessary to start his own business. This personal and professional frustration led to feelings of tension in his marriage.

Readiness (Do I Measure Up?):

Maddox felt meek, timid, and inadequate to the task he had laid out for himself. He needed to expand his skills and change his habits to meet his new personal and professional goals.

Alignment (Allies Needed):

If Maddox was going to achieve his goals, he needed an A-level support system. I advised him to identify three key individuals who could give him the direction and information he required:

1: An established entrepreneur. (Maddox selected a former colleague.)

2: Someone from his personal network, someone he trusted would give him objective feedback. (Maddox selected a cousin he grew up with, an individual who knew him since childhood.)

3: Someone to help him with his physical goals. (Maddox selected his personal trainer.)

I explained to Maddox the benefits of having the right team to gain the insights, professional skills, and physical stamina he needed to achieve his goals. Once he had this in place and felt positive about making the leap from employee to business owner, he could begin to tackle the insecurities he felt surrounding his marriage.

Vision (Making the Impossible the Possible):

Maddox needed to *mindbreak* away from the fears and anxieties that had plagued him most of his life and instead focus all of his energies on achieving his objectives. He also needed to establish professional and emotional goals that were realistic, achievable, and measurable.

With my help, Maddox developed a roadmap supporting his new personal values, which included commitment to a leadership mentality at both home and at work, greater self-respect, and increased determination. Also, in order to *mindshift* toward a leadership position, I gave him a new personal mantra: "I will raise my sail and travel toward my personal leadership to offer value to others."

Engagement (Making it Happen):

Maddox began to take control of his life by focusing on the journey, not the destination. In order to bravely *mindshift*, I instructed him to imagine himself already in a leadership role and to paint for himself a picture representing how he was leading his team. This consisted of three parts:

1. Creating and planning his new vision.

2. Empowering himself from the heart through mindful listening and committing to effective change.

3. Measuring the results and managing the risks. This also meant moving toward readiness, the second step in our BRAVE principle and accepting his new *benevoliefs*.

Throughout this process, Maddox used three key strategies to keep him on target:

The Boxing Ring Technique (discussed previously) for communication and mindful listening.

Personal anchors. (Anchors are coping techniques one can use in times of stress.) His anchors included his personal mantra, prayer/meditation, and playtime with his dog—always a judgment-free source of support.

A detailed timeline and action plan implemented according to a set schedule.

Outcomes

- Maddox acquired a new level of self-confidence.

- He regained autonomy over his career decisions.
- He learned to balance the interplay between his personal and professional lives and goals.
- Once he built a foundation for success, he was able to acquire better tools to create his plan of action for his business venture.
- He set out to acquire new skills in leadership, management, operations, and entrepreneurship that would help in his new venture.
- He developed a strategy for his family's security at the same time he cultivated and nurtured his own dreams.

As a result of our work together, Maddox's connection with his wife improved. They made a conscious decision to work on their relationship issues, including intimacy, communication and resentment. Once we had developed Maddox's new *benevolief*, it was easier for him take a personal inventory and target those areas of his behavior and thinking that needed further development. Similar to my relationship with Umesh, Maddox and his wife needed to grow both as individuals and as a couple. Eventually, however, the couples' dual *mindshifting* enhanced their communication, allowing them to achieve a new level of closeness and accountability.

What I Learned From this Client

I was reminded that personal fulfillment is not in opposition to the needs of a family. Each can support the other.

I observed the ongoing need for balance. After all, a person is the sum total of his or her inner life, including their personal relationships and career.

I witnessed how difficult it can be to get past one's anxiety, especially when it is wrapped up in guilt and fear regarding loved ones. But I observed that with the proper *mindshift*, one can conquer lifelong fears and finally achieve one's dreams.

Quote:

"Wander through it; don't worry through it. It's a better journey."

For contemplation:

Name one thing you do because someone expects you to do it, not because you want to do it. How is this keeping you from making a (needed) change?

Affirmation:

"I make the decision to live a fulfilled life."

Exercise:

We must possess a clear vision of what we seek and how to get there even if we are not sure how the outcome will play out. Design a personal journey map: draw a curved path/road on paper, adding destination points with signs of where to stop and abandon bad thoughts/habits and acquire better ones. For example, at your first stopping point, you may want to abandon "self-doubt" because it is your habitual reaction to new challenges. What would be your opposite message/action? Maybe it could be "empowering confidence"? Design an outline in which you are driving to drop off the unwanted and pick up the needed.

Chapter 6
How My Divorce Taught Me Not to be Brave

When we are children, our parents, teachers, and mentors offer us aphorisms—words of wisdom—to help us navigate life's perils. We're told "Don't judge a book by its cover," "Looks can be deceiving," and "All that glitters is not gold." These sayings carry a great deal of truth. Especially when it comes to evaluating human beings.

Many people who appear joyful and carefree on the outside are, or could be, in fact, carrying dark inner demons. For instance, someone who may present himself as strong and in control may actually feel weak and inadequate. How often do we hear stories about people who are, by all conventional standards, happy, successful, rich, and accomplished, only to then die by their own hands? The recent self-inflicted deaths of comedian Robin Williams, celebrity chef and TV travel host Anthony Bourdain, and fashion designer Kate Spade were all brutal reminders of how even individuals who appear to be leading amazing lives can find day-to-day existence unbearable.

My husband, as it turns out, became a victim of something darker. Throughout this book, I have described him as a party boy, a reveler, and an uninhibited pleasure seeker. As I later learned—and perhaps suspected for some time—his uncontrolled behavior was just a cover for a much darker side. The "business trip" he took to Las

Vegas turned out to be a wild getaway with friends. Umesh's non-stop partying took a dark turn when his companions lost track of him. When they finally found him, they brought him to a local hospital where he was put under observation and treated for an anxiety breakdown coupled with alcoholism.

"Go on without me," he later told me, sobbing on the phone after I finally learned the truth about what had happened. "I'm no good for you."

A New Diagnosis

But I wasn't about to abandon Umesh. Upon his return, we sought psychiatric treatment for him. It was during these sessions that medical professionals diagnosed Umesh as bipolar II. They made this determination based on the fact my husband had had two major depressive episodes lasting at least two weeks each, as well as one hypomanic episode. (The latter relates to an episode of euphoria not quite as extreme or severe as full-blown mania.) Importantly, according to experts, possessing such genetic tendencies can increase the risk of mood swings, depression, violence, and even suicide.

Although the medical professionals told me in no uncertain terms that Umesh suffered from a serious and potentially life-threatening condition, I refused to accept the diagnosis. I was in classic denial. I still saw Umesh as the sexy, wild-and-crazy kid I had fallen for back in high school, not the broken, bitter young man he had become. My failure to acknowledge his situation and his pain is something I regret to this day.

But even after several weeks of therapy, Umesh remained depressed and withdrawn. He fell victim to a series of illnesses, many related to his alcohol consumption, and others, I suspect, partly psychosomatic. This made it difficult for him to work. Over the next seven years, we went through a series of therapists and interventions, and the pattern was always the same. Umesh would express a strong desire for help. He would be given exercises or medications, or other therapeutic techniques designed to alleviate his symptoms, leading him to the road of recovery. He'd even adhere to the prescribed regimen for perhaps one or two weeks. But then the effort would prove too great and he would backslide.

Once he slipped up, he would return to old habits. Eventually, I would realize he had relapsed, forcing a series of emotional and painful recriminations. Umesh would then beg for forgiveness—or lash out at me, depending on his mood—and the whole awful cycle would begin anew. We were living in our very own substance-fueled, nightmarish version of *Groundhog Day,* with Umesh and me fated to experience the same chain of events on an endless loop.

So, why did I stick with him? I often asked myself this same question, and each time, I returned to the same answer. I believed—I honestly believed—that if I just held on long enough, things would improve. I know this sounds like the definition of insanity: doing the same thing over and over again, and each time expecting a different result. But I was ignoring this admonishment in favor of the even simpler saying, "If at first you don't succeed, try, try again."

What did I say earlier about aphorisms?

Passage to India

After each failure, Umesh and I would regroup, try to determine where we had failed, and conceive of yet another way to attack his problem. But the more we talked, the more we disagreed, leading to fights resulting in mutual feelings of hopelessness, exhaustion, and emptiness. In time it became clear Umesh needed to a find a new way back to health. And I needed to find a way to cope until he did.

I asked Umesh to leave our home. I felt hopeless, guilty, and saddened as I realized our problems were bigger than the both of us. It was decided that distance and separation might be a plausible resolution for the time being. At the same time, our financial situation was in the negative, so I borrowed $2,000 from my mother and bought a round-trip ticket to Bangalore, India. Umesh had seen a therapist—let's call him Dr. Khatri—with whom both of us had connected to early in his treatment. Dr. Khatri ran a center specializing in the use of yoga and naturopathy to promote physical and mental health in Bangalore, a megacity of more than 10 million people.

There were several reasons we felt going to this center was a good idea. First, Dr. Khatri said he could collaborate with us, both jointly and individually, to provide the needed coaching and tools to deal with our increasingly desperate situation. Second, I felt compelled to connect with the land of my ancestors. Having visited India several times as an adult, I believed this 5,000-year-old civilization—one which had given rise to Jainism, Hinduism, Sikhism, and Buddhism—held the key to my spiritual salvation. Finally, I had to get out of Orange County. There were just too many associations here, too many triggers, pushing us back into old patterns and habits. I figured going halfway around the world might grant me the perspective and clarity to get our lives back on track.

Umesh left first for Bangalore, undergoing three weeks of individualized treatment before I joined him for my own regimen of customized therapy. Although this was not my first visit to India, I still felt a jolt of culture shock when I departed the airport by taxi and headed into the city. The sheer mass of humanity was overwhelming. I had spent some time in both Chicago and Los Angeles, and while the freeway traffic in both cities is the stuff of legend, once you get off the major roads and highways, moving about freely is rarely an issue.

Not so in Bangalore. It's wall-to-wall people, cars, buses, and bicycles wherever you go. The city smells different, too, blending the noxious odor of vehicle exhaust with the pungent odors of native cooking and water pollution. The architecture is stunning, an eclectic mix of ornate British Imperial palaces, monochrome mid-20th century apartment buildings, and wildly futuristic office towers straight out of a science fiction movie.

Although situated in the heart of bustling Bangalore, Dr. Khatri's center felt remote and peaceful. There, he and his staff introduced me to a wide range of life-altering tools, including dietary changes, yoga instruction, meditation, and individualized marriage and relationship therapy. Umesh and I also encountered a South Indian saint who offered us a unique perspective on life and its meaning. (I have kept in touch with this venerable guru ever since, and he's had a major impact on my ability to behave bravely.)

Happily, the therapy—which lasted several weeks— was nothing short of life altering, resulting in a major *mindshift* for us both. Before I went to India, I believed many of my problems were the fault of Umesh, his bipolarism, and his addictions. Now I understood that if I were ever to heal, I had to change my own patterns first, especially my beliefs and expectations. This revelation led to a major spiritual reawakening that Umesh sensed, too.

Homecoming

Returning to Orange County, Umesh and I decided to live separately as we worked to implement the healing and growth techniques we had learned in India. Sanam lived with me, although Umesh would visit her regularly. (She would later stay with him during her summer vacation.) My daily routine consisted of getting her dressed, taking her to the park, and later, when she got a bit older, to preschool. Throughout the day, I made certain Sanam was rarely out of sight.

During this period, I continued speaking with my good friend, Amisha. She provided the empathy and sympathy I needed to carry on. Not only that, but she also offered useful advice. For example, she recommended I avoid topics and issues I knew would antagonize Umesh, and not to respond whenever he tried baiting me into arguments. I had three other friends I found I could turn to as well, but while I was always able to take comfort in their company, I soon found myself again searching for answers. And despite the insights I had gained in India, I continued to view many of my actions through the prism of how they would affect Umesh. And the more I focused on him, the more I lost my sense of self.

As time went on, Umesh and I continued going to individual therapy. (We no longer sought help as a couple.) When one therapist didn't work out, we'd try another. Between us, we saw five different therapists over an eight-year period. Each provided some tool, insight, or takeaway

I found valuable, but none offered the comprehensive solution we so desperately desired. (The penultimate therapist we saw suggested I pursue a hobby, something I could do just for myself. This led me to learn the *tabla*, an Indian percussion instrument I had always found fascinating.)

Emotional Affairs

While Umesh and I had many issues, one of them was *not* the issue that destroys so many marriages: *infidelity.* As far as I know, while he often drank to excess, could not control his spending, and often preferred to spend his free time with his buddies instead of with me and Sanam, Umesh never cheated on me.

Of course, not all affairs are sexual. There is such a thing as "emotional cheating." Emotional cheating is rarely talked about. You almost never see it portrayed in movies or TV shows. It's not nearly as salacious or scandalous as traditional sexual infidelity. It never leads to unwanted pregnancies or illegitimate children. But an emotional affair can be just as destructive as a sexual one. Perhaps even more so. Because while a sexual affair can always be dismissed with "It didn't mean anything," the power—and danger—of an emotional affair is the fact that, by its very nature, it *does* mean something.

An emotional affair is one in which a married individual turns to someone else for emotional support and emotional intimacy. This other person becomes the sounding board for you to discuss your hopes, dreams, fears, and desires. The "other" in an emotional affair is more than just a "friend." He/she becomes an intimate confidante. A confessor. You know you're having an emotional affair when you realize you'd rather spend time with this individual than your own spouse.

And here, I have to confess that I bear some guilt. For while I have no evidence that Umesh ever cheated on me sexually, I did indeed cheat on Umesh emotionally. Twice.

The first affair began in 2002. I had just started working in HR for a national health care company. One of my clients, an internal customer, was a vice president of sales. Let's call him "Jake." When I started in my role, he asked to meet me to discuss hiring needs.

We met in the hallway outside his office. He was in his late 30s. Caucasian. Tall. Brown-eyed, with close-cropped brown hair that was just starting to show flecks of grey. His custom-tailored suit perfectly complemented his slim, athletic frame. He offered his hand, and I shook it. His grip was firm but friendly. Just like a salesperson's handshake should be. Immediately, our eyes locked. I felt an immediate attraction. From the look in his eyes, I could sense that he felt it, too.

Over the next year, Jake and I worked together regularly. And I have to admit, I was crushing on him pretty hard. When we talked on the phone, we'd always drift from business matters to our personal lives. Every few weeks, we'd go out to lunch and talk about our families, our interests, and our frustrations. I felt completely relaxed around him. So much so that I occasionally flirted outright with him.

But it never went further than that. Not that I didn't fantasize about him sexually. I did. But he was married. I was married. Whenever I thought of Jake and me getting together, I thought about my daughter and what the revelation of an affair might do to her. And I thought of my family. No one on either my father's side or my mother's had ever divorced. In the conservative Indian culture in which I was raised, such a thing was unthinkable! (Strangely, I never factored Umesh into this. We had ceased being intimate some time ago.)

I like to think that I was too noble to pursue Jake physically, but the fact is, I was just too scared. My desires, as strong as they were, were overruled by my fears. Which, in retrospect, was probably a good thing. There's a reason humans invented guilt. It often prevents us from doing things we would most certainly regret later.

My second emotional affair occurred eight years later. Let's call him "Sanjay." An Indian-American of about 40, he was applying for an executive role with one of my clients. I interviewed him as I would any other job candidate. I found him to be intelligent. Charming. Funny. Though I gave him a solid recommendation, alas, he did not get the position. However, a few weeks later, he emailed me to go out for coffee. He said he wanted to network. I agreed. We met several mornings later at a nearby restaurant and basically talked shop. We exchanged business cards and I offered him leads on other possible job opportunities. After that, we continued to keep in touch via email, as I did with many of my other contacts.

Then, a few weeks later, Sanjay invited me out to dinner. I suspected he was interested in me personally, and I flashed back to my "near miss" with Jake eight years prior. Still, I was flattered. More than that, I was curious. I was intrigued. So I agreed to the "date."

We met at one of South County's higher-end restaurants. It turned out, we had a lot in common, and I freely shared a lot of personal information with him. By this time, I was already legally separated from Umesh — more about this shortly — so I did not feel the same degree of guilt I had when I went out with Jake. But I was not ready to get intimately involved with someone who was not my husband. Especially not a married man.

We continued to see each other for several times thereafter. During one of these "dates," Sanjay told me that his wife was possibly seeing another man. At this point, I realized we were relying on each other for emotional comfort and solace. I also recognized we were quickly heading down a path that could lead to some very complicated, perhaps even messy, entanglements. My relationship with Umesh was not yet resolved, and the last thing I needed now was to complicate things further. So, as gently as I could, I ended the relationship.

In either of these cases, did I "cheat" on Umesh? I think a good lawyer could argue otherwise. However, from a purely ethical standpoint, I believe I did. A marriage isn't just about monogamous sex. It's about a deep and lasting emotional connection. It's about having shared values ambitions, being there to support the other in times of need. If someone else is filling these latter roles, it greatly diminishes the quality of the marriage. I take full responsibility for my actions in this area, and only take comfort in the fact I did not pursue these relationships further than I did.

Step by Step

Before our eventual separation, back when Sanam was about 5 years old, Umesh returned to his alcoholic ways with a vengeance. Realizing the direness of the situation, some helpful family members and I staged an intervention. Confronting Umesh in his living room, we expressed our love for him, but also our distress over his self-destructiveness. When it was my turn to speak, I confessed his drinking made me feel angry, desperate, and often hopeless. I was careful to emphasize I did not want to divorce him but needed him to get better so we could return to the life we had when we were first married.

Feeling both the pressure and the support from all of us, Umesh agreed to seek help from Alcoholics Anonymous (AA). He began attending local AA groups at various South County locations on and off for about a month. Whenever I asked about these meetings, he would shrug them off or insist the goings-on were "confidential." But then one day he surprised me by bringing home a pamphlet for the O.C. chapter of Al-Anon and suggested I go.

I immediately balked at this. *He was the one with the problem,* I thought. Why should I go? He explained that Al-Anon is a support group for people affected by a family member's drinking. (Apparently, he had heard about Al-Anon from a fellow AA member and believed I could benefit from it.) Because Umesh had agreed to join AA, I agreed to give Al-Anon a try.

Little did I know at the time how much this group would change my life. My first task was to learn about Al-Anon: where it held its meetings and what I could expect once I arrived. For those of you who don't know about this amazing organization, it was founded in 1951 by two women known only as Anne B. and Lois W., the latter being the wife of AA co-founder Bill W.

Unlike AA, the group is not designed to help addicts, but instead provide support for families of individuals who abuse alcohol and drugs. In fact, the group's literature specifically defines alcoholism as a "family illness" that damages non-drinking family members as much as it does the addicts themselves. It adheres to the same 12-step program developed for AA, but in step 12 replaces the word "alcoholics" with the word "others." I saw nothing but possible benefits in sharing my thoughts, hopes, and fears with others who were dealing with a challenge similar to my own.

I attended my first Al-Anon meeting on a Monday evening at a church in the city of Tustin. Admittedly, I was nervous and didn't know what to expect. Held in a small room, roughly a dozen chairs were arranged in a circle. Just like in the movies I'd seen, there was a table set to the side for coffee and pastries. All of the people I met greeted me warmly. They represented a virtual cross-section of the city's diverse population, with the genders divided almost equally between men and women.

As a new guest, I was invited to introduce myself—first name only, of course—and to explain why I had come. I told my story in as much detail as I dared, but before I could even get halfway through, I broke down crying. At the end of the meeting, a 40ish red-haired woman approached me with a hug.

"Thank you," I said, feeling sheepish for my tears, yet grateful for this stranger's warmth.

Her name was Katie, and she offered to become my "sponsor," the person I could turn to in times of need, day or night. I apologized for my breakdown, but Katie insisted I had done well that night.

"If you're sharing, you're working," she told me.

This was certainly news to me, and it made me feel even better about my decision to come here.

As Katie and I continued to talk, she advised me to enroll in the group's 12-step program. "Seriously," she said, "It's just as effective for family members as it is for the abusers themselves." Still, she warned me this was an arduous, time-consuming process. Should I need help along the way, she promised to be there for me just as her sponsor had been when she joined the group five years prior.

"You can't do it alone. Nobody can."

I told her I was ready to accept any help I could get.

The next day, I was out jogging when Katie called me. After asking me how I was doing, I launched into a litany of complaints about Umesh. Like my old guru back in India, Katie insisted she couldn't help me if I continued to focus on Umesh and his behavior.

"You needed to get out of *his* head and into your own."

Such sagacious advice convinced me Al-Anon could be my path to salvation, and I ended up going to meeting after meeting. It soon became my rock, my home away from home. And Katie and the other members became my surrogate family. In some ways, we connected more deeply than my real one because we shared not blood, but life experiences. We knew each other's stories in ways even our parents and siblings never could. Katie soon advised me to become group treasurer, her way of making sure I continued to attend meetings. Her suggestion worked because I never missed another that year.

Thanks to Katie's support, I made it through all 12 steps:

- I admitted I was powerless over Umesh's alcoholism, and that my life had become unmanageable.
- I turned my will and life over to the care of God.
- I made a searching and fearless moral inventory of myself.
- I admitted to God, to myself, and to Al-Anon, the exact nature of my wrongs.
- I became entirely ready to have God remove all my character defects.
- I made a list of persons I believe I had harmed and vowed to make amends to them all.

- I made direct amends to such people wherever possible—including my parents, friends, and yes, even Umesh.
- I continued to take a personal inventory and when I was wrong, promptly admitted it.
- I sought through prayer and meditation to improve my conscious contact with God, praying only for knowledge of God's will for me and the power to carry it out.
- Receiving a spiritual awakening as a result of these steps, I tried to carry this message to others and to practice these principles in all of my affairs.

The Reality of Divorce

In spite of the progress I made in Al-Anon and the other efforts to positively transform my life, by spring 2013, I knew it was over between Umesh and me. Our relationship had run its course. It sounds strange to say this, but the good news was both Umesh and I had sufficiently recovered enough to divorce. Still, over the years, people have asked me why I decided to split at this time, when both he and I were "doing better."

The reason is simple. Divorce is brutal. The upheaval can destroy the weak and the vulnerable. Both parties must be strong and capable to survive. It had been clear to me for years that Umesh and I had no future together, but I wanted to stay true to my vows, and didn't want to put Sanam through the trauma. In addition, I feared that if I initiated proceedings earlier, he might relapse. So I waited until I felt we were both ready for the emotional, spiritual, and financial impact a divorce would trigger.

Not that I didn't still feel guilty about what I was doing. I kept thinking about all of the people who would be affected by this decision: our family members, our friends—but most of all, Sanam. I waited so long because I wanted to make sure she had the emotional maturity to handle it. I needed her to not just think, *but to know*, this was the best thing for all of us—that struggling to stay together for the sake of appearances or maintaining some semblance of "normalcy" was only delaying the inevitable.

When I announced my decision to Umesh, he asked for a year to think about it. I agreed to his request for a delay. That he was hesitating suggested he saw our future quite differently than I did. I understood his reticence. After all, I was his life preserver, the person he could always count on to rescue him when he got in over his head. (His words, not mine.) Letting me go meant he was now wholly responsible for himself. And I'm sure that frightened him terribly. Because it frightened me, too.

The following spring, I asked Umesh for a decision. He graciously agreed to the divorce. A few months later, we signed the necessary papers. That was it. Our marriage was over. Disappointment, shame, fear, and sadness filled Umesh and me. After all, we had spent much of our lives together, and now that was all in the past. But underneath all these negative feelings, a faint but palpable sense of hope also began to emerge. I had finally turned the page on what had been a harrowing chapter of my life's journey. What such a significant change would bring, I couldn't say. But I was eager to find out.

*****

In the following section, we will explore the story of my client who also experienced a challenging marriage that threatened to dismantle her self-identity and led to years of unhappiness. It's my hope that by sharing it with you, it will offer some insights on how to behave bravely in the face of matrimonial adversity.

Case Study: Laila

Laila is a Middle Eastern woman from the United Arab Emirates (UAE) who married an American and has been living in the United States for several years. When I met her in 2017, she had just quit a fabulous job at PepsiCo as a sustainability/environmental manager—requiring her to travel and work long hours—to focus on her husband and 3-year-old daughter. The couple had just moved to Orange County so she could be closer to her brother in Irvine.

But then life threw her a major curve ball. She learned her husband had, for years, been cheating on her with their housekeeper. Shaken and furious, her anger was so palpable she could barely contain it at times. A driven professional with an indomitable will, she refused to succumb to negativity. Instead, she threw herself into focusing on two major goals:

1. Managing the anger, sadness, and resentment she harbored over her husband's affair.
2. Landing a new job that would allow her to work closer to home so she could be present for her young daughter.

State of Mind

When I first began working with Laila, she was still reeling from her husband's betrayal. Angry, fearful, and resentful, she wanted to "get even" with her husband. This meant breaking him down, ridiculing him, and disrespecting him so he would suffer like she did.

Situation

Laila possessed serious life/career issues that threatened to disrupt her equilibrium and life outlook. Having discovered her husband's infidelity, she now contemplated divorce, yet was confused about the prospect. She also felt conflicted between her professional ambitions and maternal responsibilities.

Status

Laila was emotionally torn and intellectually confused. She felt she needed new tools to cope with her mounting anger and frustration.

Being BRAVE

Beliefs >>> *Benevoliefs* (I'm a Sexy Woman):

At times, Laila blamed herself for her husband's affair. Her (limiting) belief told her she wasn't sexy or attractive enough for him to be interested in her. Her doubts about her femininity and attractiveness went back decades. Growing up in a culture where males and females were most often segregated, she had, as a child, little experience with boys. Like all women in this socially rigid society, she led a segregated existence. To compensate for her perceived lack of beauty and desirability, she focused on her studies and professional achievement throughout her early years without ever cultivating a strong sexual identity.

Readiness (Shedding What Longer Serves):

I wanted Laila to understand—and believe—that she was, indeed, sexy, attractive, desirable, and worthy of love. To help her develop a more positive self-image—to reveal her "inner girl" and validate her sexuality—I suggested using what I call "The Pretend Strategy."

This involves assuming the persona of the individual one wants to become, acting in character until it becomes part of who you really are. (In other words, "Fake it 'til you make it.") This is similar to a *benevolief,* but involves action, not just visualization. To achieve this *mindshift,* I worked to reset Laila's rage-fueled thinking with more positive messages, focusing on establishing healthier habits. I wanted her to learn how to validate herself by looking not at her outward, physical appearance, but inward at her behavior, attitude, and values.

Simultaneously, I advised Laila to employ the Forgiveness Technique. We are often told forgiveness is required if we are ever to transcend the pain of past traumas. Similar to ideas put forth in Al-Anon and AA, the first step is to identify the individual (or individuals) you believe have wronged you. To this end, I asked Laila to write a letter covering three topics:

1. The relationship she wanted to repair.
2. An acknowledgement of her part in the conflict in which she wished to make amends.
3. A statement in which she clearly expressed her desire to forgive.

The above very much aligns with the Readiness and Vision part of the BRAVE principles. Often, we are not ready to rebuild our relationships, yet forgiveness can be an essential first step. In Laila's case, forgiveness would allow her to see things from her husband's perspective, promoting healing within her.

I also counseled Laila to employ The Sun Ray Technique to remind herself of those qualities that initially attracted her to her husband. I asked her to draw a large circle with sun rays emanating from it. I then had her write her husband's name in the center of the circle. On each sun ray she listed an attribute she admired about him: intelligence, confidence, sense of humor, etc.

As a result of participating in the above exercises, as well as doing crucial self-work, Laila was at last able to recognize her husband's affair wasn't all about her but was instead rooted in many of his own issues. This epiphany forced a little opening in her thinking, leading her to adapt a new attitude of compassion.

Alignment (My New Style):

Laila updated her personal "brand"—not only her choice of clothes and makeup, but also her interests, hobbies, and priorities. Working together we ensured these choices weren't arbitrary or based on others' expectations but were expressions of her truest desires.

Vision (I, Talented):

Laila needed specific aspirations that would help her cope more successfully with life's challenges. By having a clearer vision of where her life was headed, she could place short-term setbacks and disappointments into better perspective. She also needed help designing a better job search strategy. She had to clearly "see" the type of position she desired, the work she wanted to do, and the affects her activities would have on herself, her family, and on the larger world.

Engagement (My High Heels):

Together, we designed and implemented steps to launch Laila's career search. After mapping specific goals, we developed strategies for supporting her financial needs while developing a sustainable work/life balance.

I helped her make better personal and financial decisions, including creating a monthly savings plan, in the event she would have to weather a divorce. Through my tutelage, Laila learned a number of valuable techniques to help her build stronger interpersonal relationships.

In particular, she discovered how to accept and cultivate her own vulnerability, both personally and professionally. As part of the above, we also instituted a gentle morning workout routine that included listening to music to quiet her mind and relieve stress. I also suggested Laila begin keeping a daily journal to tamp down rage triggers.

Strategy

Now that we had a series of personal/professional goals, we developed a road map to achieve them. Focusing first on the personal, my primary objective was to make Laila aware of her rage mindset. To do this, I focused on creating good habits to inform her daily routine. I also introduced new self-validation techniques to reframe her self-image and definition of beauty. Encouraging her to return to her personal vision statement on a daily basis, I emphasized repeated reinforcement to strengthen her *mindshift*. Ultimately, I wanted her to be enthusiastic about who she was and what her life could become.

I believed that if Laila could make herself feel good physically, the other changes would be less difficult to achieve. As noted earlier, Laila biggest challenge involved forgiving her husband for having the affair. Forgiveness would free her to move forward, not just in her personal life, but her professional one, too.

Under my direction, Laila did the following to advance her career:

- Identified target companies in the environmental sector offering local positions that didn't require overnight traveling. (If she could secure such a position, she could better take care of her daughter, yet build a financial nest egg so that if she chose to, she could file for divorce.)
- Redesigned her resume to emphasize metrics of successes she had achieved: e.g. the number of dollars she had saved her past employer, the additional income received as a result of her efforts, the percentage drop in customer complaints, etc. (This, I believed, was more compelling to read than vague, clichéd statements about "developing creative solutions" and/or "being a team player.")
- Created an action schedule to formalize her employment outreach campaign. This required Laila to identify X number of potential employers every day, to send out X number of resumes, and connect with X number of contacts per week. (Social networking was also important, especially on LinkedIn and Facebook.) She was therefore required to reach out to X number friends—and to friends of friends—every day, unapologetically enlisting their help in her job search.

Steps Taken:

Per our program, Laila began each day with a workout routine supported by music. This allowed her to focus her mind and prepare herself for the day ahead.

Once she had completed her routine, Laila would make an entry in her journal describing her feelings and state of mind. Before starting her new regimen, the first thing Laila thought of when she awoke was her husband's affair. This grief caused her to begin each day in a state of rage. Many mornings, she dealt with this rage by confronting its source—her husband—leading to a predictable exchange of accusations and recriminations. I instead suggested that she start each day in such a way to dissipate this rage and help her avoid confrontations that would inevitably lead to more anger and pain. (In fact, this new approach seemed to have precisely this desired effect, as reflected in the increasing positive entries she put in her journal.)

To ensure Laila stuck to her plan, I asked her to make a weekly appointment with herself. Its purpose: To help her discover her inner girl. Once a week, she was to go to her favorite spa or department store and experiment with makeup and fashion choices, something she had never done in previous years. I also wanted her to study sex. She could access anything to open her eyes to the pleasures, opportunities, and romantic variety she had for so long missed out on.

Her husband complained that Laila never smiled. So, she ventured to the makeup counter at one of South Coast Plaza's high-end department stores. There, she tried a variety of lipsticks and literally practiced smiling in a mirror. This was to cultivate Laila's inner girl and increase her sexual confidence. (Why? We must feel sexy inside before we can convey our appeal to others.)

Again, to bring out Laila's inner girl, we worked on developing playfulness and flirtation. Like all women, Laila wanted to be adored. Since childhood, she had been trained to believe such feelings were inappropriate. We needed desperately to *mindbreak* her from that repressive attitude, and *mindshift* her into a position of empowerment.

Laila implemented the professional job search protocols we designed and stuck to the schedule. As a result, she received numerous inquiries from companies meeting her criteria, landed several successful interviews, and received a lucrative job offer at the company where she continues to work to this day.

Outcomes

Laila has lost 10 pounds and is maintaining a very balanced exercise/meditation program.

Laila is much clearer about her life goals.

Laila has become much better about reducing her feelings of rage. She has not completely forgiven her husband, but she has become more comfortable with herself and her own ability to change the way she feels about outside triggers.

What I Learned from this Client

I recognized the rage and fear my own marriage once caused within me. For me, it was only through working with Umesh that we were able to arrive at a harmonious solution.

I was reminded of the need for gentleness and compassion in intimate relationships.

I discovered the ongoing nature of recovery from grief and pain, something I am still working on to this day.

Quote:

"The reflection we have for ourselves is part of what makes us beautiful."

For contemplation

Describe a time in your life when you felt betrayed. What did you do? How did you feel?

Affirmation:

"I uncover a new inner beauty in forgiveness."

Exercise:

Feeling betrayed can be short-lived, and you can make sure it's temporary by choosing to make it so. But don't discount the fact betrayal contains a strong sense of loss. Before you can let it go, you will need time to grieve. To do so, embark on the following:

Work on moving past your own barriers with a trusted mentor or coach.

Keep a strong focus on your personal health and well-being.

Decide if your relationship is worth continuing despite the betrayal.

Connect and express with "I" statements reflecting objectively what you need the other person to understand. (If you are unable to communicate, try to write a letter and/or get your grief under control via a journal and/or a forgiveness letter to move past your hurt.)

Chapter 7
How I Learned to Be BRAVE

In AA, members are told they usually must hit "rock bottom" before finding the urgency—and courage—to turn their lives around. For some, this means losing their personal possessions, their house, their car, their savings—as a consequence of substance abuse. For others, it can mean waking up in an abandoned tenement in a rough part of town bruised and bloodied with no memory of how they got there. And for others still, it can mean the pain and humiliation of being arrested, booked, and spending time in jail alongside others who have taken a wrong turn in life.

As I learned in Al-Anon, alcoholism and drug abuse can affect family members just as seriously as it does the offenders themselves. Little wonder we tend to travel the same downward path as those who are using and abusing. All of this is to say, I, too, needed to hit my bottom: divorce. Signing court papers was to me the equivalent of signing a criminal confession. It was me admitting before the world I had failed at my most important task: being a successful wife and mother. The shame I felt was palpable. I wanted nothing more than to run away to some town on the other side of the country, a place where no one knew me.

Suffering this way led me to thoughts about reincarnation, a concept central to the beliefs of Jainists, Hindus, and Buddhists alike. I wanted to be reborn, to receive a fresh start—so long as this other life still somehow involved being near my Sanam. Of course, the ancient faiths I mentioned also believe in *karma*, the idea our past deeds not only come back to bless or haunt us in this life, but also in future lives. If this were the case, then even reincarnation could not free me from the spiritual agony I felt. If I were to redeem myself, if I were going to claw my way out of the emotional black hole into which I had fallen, it would have to be through my own efforts, not the result of some metaphysical do-over.

Where Everybody Knows Your Name

Back in the 1980s, I used to watch the NBC sitcom *Cheers*. (Didn't everybody?) Set in a Boston bar "where everybody knows your name," the show featured a cast of eclectic characters who bonded as a surrogate family. They could always be counted on to support the others in times of trouble, even when the calamities were self-inflicted. After my divorce, I longed for my Sam Malone, my Diane Chambers, or even my Cliff Clavin. The fact was, although I had now lived in Irvine for many years, I had made zero friends in my neighborhood.

Yes, I knew most of my immediate neighbors on a passing basis, but beyond trading comments about the weather, I knew little about them and they knew little about me. These weren't people I might ask to collect my mail when I was out of town let alone attempt to commiserate with about something as serious as the demise of a marriage.

Outside of my loving family, for whom I remain ever grateful, and the handful of individuals with whom I'd grown close in Al-Anon, I had little in the way of what you might call an "emotional support system." Going about my day often meant seeing other mothers sitting at the park talking and laughing with each other. Observing such a scene couldn't fail to sadden me, especially when I watched their children playing together on the playground. Witnessing the easy manner in which they interacted made me feel inferior. Like an outsider.

Meanwhile, at work, my job often filled me with worry and anxiety. I was basically living paycheck to paycheck, and constantly worried something might go wrong. Just a single slipup, a wrong word, an inappropriate glance, could force both Sanam and me out of our house and onto the streets. (Although Orange County is world-famous for its affluence, it is not immune from the homeless problem plaguing nearly every American metropolis.) Ultimately, seeing other people's happiness, whether it be at home or work, just deepened my depression. I didn't want to be a downer. I didn't want to be sad, but I didn't know what else to do.

Salvation in 12 Not-So-Easy Steps

They say God doesn't give you any problems you can't handle, but sometimes I can't help wondering if that's true. I can think of tens of millions of victims of war, disease, famine, and criminal violence who might beg to differ. Still, in my case, I was fortunate to get the help I needed when I needed it most.

Al-Anon turned out to be my primary lifeline. The support I received there was invaluable. *They were my friends.* I can honestly say I would not be where I am today if not for this organization, which sustained me in my darkest moments. Likewise, the level of empathy and encouragement I continuously received was nothing short of awe-inspiring. As I recounted in the last chapter, my sponsor, Katie, helped me get through my first 12-step regimen when I was trying to salvage my marriage. After my divorce, part of me felt like an alcoholic who'd fallen off the wagon and needed to start anew. Back to step 1. Again, Katie served as my rock, catching me whenever I found myself slipping, too overwhelmed by it all.

Although designed for alcoholics, the 12 steps are, in my opinion, so well thought out and universally applicable they can assist any individual who is crying out for help. My life experience continues to affirm we are all flawed in one way or another. We are all vulnerable to any number of temptations compelling us to ignore our better judgments and follow our urges, however self-destructive they may be.

For some people, their weakness is alcohol. For others, its chemical stimulants, including nicotine. Some are compulsive gamblers or have sexual addictions. And we all know workaholics, people who are compulsive about keeping busy, even if it means ignoring friends and family. Heck, some people are even addicted to 12-step programs. Seriously. Parodied in the movie, *Fight Club*, these individuals run obsessively from one meeting to another, drawing a rush from the emotional ride. They can even experience painful psychological withdrawal if they can't find their next meeting.

The more I began attending Monday night gatherings of Al-Anon, the more I became aware of my own part in trying to control and manipulate Umesh in the belief, as heartfelt as it might have seemed to me, I was doing the "right" thing for us. (As I eventually learned, you can never achieve a full understanding of, or be comfortable with, the disease of alcoholism.) Working with Katie and other group members, I learned how relinquishing control—one of the hardest things a person like me can do—can actually be empowering. Surrendering the need to be in charge and/or responsible for someone else is downright liberating. Allowing Umesh to make his own decisions, his own mistakes, and to be wholly responsible for the consequences, allowed me to experience euphoric freedom.

As I progressed through the 12 steps, Katie was not just my sponsor, but also my confidant. I looked forward to seeing her at every Al-Anon meeting. Once, when I expressed my feelings of fear and anxiety, she recommended I write a letter to myself. In it, I was to reveal a secret I dared not admit to anyone. That night, after much soul searching, I recalled a memory from a childhood so painful I had never even discussed it with any of my therapists.

In the letter, I described the incident in as much detail as I could recall, as well as the emotions I associated with it. The next day, Katie asked to see the document. With great reluctance I pulled it from my purse, offering it to her. She did not take it. Instead, she handed me a lighter and instructed me to burn the letter.

"Why?" I asked, confused.

"Because it will make you feel better."

So, with trembling hands, I flicked on the lighter. Carefully, I lowered the folded letter into the dancing flame, then watched as the fire began to consume the paper. At the last possible moment, I released it, letting it flutter to the ground, where I stomped out what remained with my shoe. Then I paused for a moment to consider what had just occurred.

Katie was right. I did feel better.

More on "Letting Go"

The first step in all 12-step programs is "letting go." I mean, really LETTING GO. This was not natural for me.

And I suspect it's not natural for most people. When it comes to our lives, as might be expected, most of us are control freaks. We like to be in charge of all aspects. When we get up. When we go to bed. What we eat. What we drink. What we wear. What books and blogs we read. What shows and movies we watch on television.

Understandably, one of the biggest sources of friction in any marriage can occur when one partner believes the other is trying to "control" him/her. But when it comes to breaking dependence, whether it be chemical or emotional, relinquishing control over yourself and others is essential. And, as I discovered, while not easy, it's something that can be learned over time.

While I was busy acquiring this skill, I really was living one day at a time.

I had no idea as to my end goal. No fixed objective. As you might imagine, this was uncomfortable for me. I always feared the unknown—and what could be more unknown than the future?

With no specific goal in mind, I often found it difficult to follow Katie's guidance. It was difficult to tamp down my urge to demand a reason for every action or a clear chain of cause-and-effect for every event. Wrapping my head around surrendering to the universe was truly a challenge for me. What I eventually discovered is that working toward a singular goal can be self-defeating. Not only is there a good chance you'll never achieve your desired outcome, but also tunnel vision can blind you to other opportunities along the way. As so many philosophers have said, it is the journey, not the goal, that is truly important.

With sustained effort, I learned to no longer obsess over what it is I believed I wanted or needed. I now viewed God or fate or kismet or whatever we choose to call life's guiding force as something working silently behind the scenes. Tasked with ensuring what is needed to appear at just the right time, somehow things work out the way they should. (In spite of our doubts, worries and misgivings.) As for my own participation in life's unfolding, I did my best to keep my "side of the street" clean, focusing on what I can actually control: my thinking, my behavior, my choices, and how I treat others. This epiphany was so powerful and liberating it became one of the pillars of my coaching.

Turning Things Around

With the help of Al-Anon, I learned to transform my anxiety into motivation. During the day, I threw myself into my work, determined to be the most responsible, productive professional I could be. In my role as senior talent acquisition for my company's HR department, I learned and put into practice the coaching skills that eventually led me to the position I hold today. After hours, I relieved tension through playing the *tabla*, the traditional Indian drums I had acquired while married to Umesh, and also began the study of *feng shui*, the ancient Chinese art of optimizing the flow of life energy (qi) through spatial arrangement. At home and at work, I took care to ensure my surroundings were arranged to produce the most positive emotional response.

I also rededicated myself to a regimen of proper diet and exercise. For the first time, I hired a personal trainer who designed a workout especially for my needs and abilities, while also holding me accountable. I began researching expert information on natural health options. As the saying goes, "You are what you eat," and my usual diet of convenient, processed foods had been doing me little good, physically, mentally, or emotionally.

Determined to transform my life from the inside out, I vowed to eat simply and naturally, incorporating more organic fruits, vegetables, and legumes into a more balanced diet. After just a week, I felt a difference in my mood and energy level. (Over the course of several years, I actually lost 30 pounds!) Also, my sleep improved. Instead of tossing, turning, and waking up a half-dozen times a night, I found I could fall asleep quickly until awakened by my alarm. Beyond just eating better, it's amazing what a solid eight hours of sleep can do for a troubled soul.

A New Approach to Therapy

In addition to these lifestyle changes, I revised my approach to therapy and self-help. For more than a decade, I had been in and out of professional couples and individual therapy, the only tangible result being my divorce. Of course, when I started going with Umesh, I did not think I needed any major improvements aside from finding ways to better deal with his bipolar behavior.

In the end, all my work seemed to come back to the same mantra: *Stop focusing on Umesh and start focusing on yourself.* Even my trip to India, as enlightening as it had been, ended with me convinced that if I just stopped seeing everything as a function of Umesh's shortcomings, my life would improve. Soon after my divorce, I discovered how wrong I had been. My problem wasn't just my focus on Umesh; my problem was *me.*

Not that I wholly blamed my prior therapists for what sounds like a misdiagnosis. The signs had been there all along; I had just failed to heed them. Looking back, one of my first therapists called me a "rescuer," someone who finds validation in "fixing" broken people. Others had focused on my co-dependency and my skewed view of men in general as both protectors and abusers. Not that all the so-called experts got it right. One told me I didn't know how to be a "sexy girlfriend" and advised me to stop cooking for my husband—and any subsequent boyfriends—as this put me in the role of mother rather than sexual partner. Looking back, I have to laugh at how seriously I once took these therapists' diagnoses and advice.

I also discovered having a support group to be essential for personal healing. As much as Americans like to talk about the virtues of "rugged individualism," the fact is, each one of us is stronger *together*. Sociologists have long spoken about what's called "the wisdom of the crowd," how large groups of people tend to possess information that is both broader, deeper, and more accurate than even the most educated individual can muster.

Examples from popular culture and academia reflect this same truth. Researchers studying the results on the TV game show, *Who Wants to Be a Millionaire?* discovered stumped contestants who chose the "Ask the Audience" lifeline rather than the "Phone a Friend" option received a significantly higher percentage of correct answers, even when the designated friend was highly educated and/or an expert in a particular field. That no one is completely alone in their personal struggles, that we all depend on one another, is one of the key insights I gained during this difficult period. It was the *ah-ha* moment I experienced in my immediate post-divorce experience.

As strange as this may sound, I am grateful for the pain Umesh put me through. (Umesh has said the same about *me!*) Diamonds are formed when ordinary carbon is put under immense heat and pressure, and plant and animal species evolve when pressured to do so. Likewise,

I could not have developed so much emotionally without experiencing the anguish of learning what does *not* serve me. Consciously or unconsciously, the love of my life served as the catalyst for my journey of self-discovery.

Becoming a Life Coach

Maybe you have heard stories about people who went on to become doctors or medical researchers due to being sick as children or losing a loved one to disease at an early age. Perhaps you have read about individuals who signed up to be police officers or state prosecutors after losing a family member to crime. It turns out, trauma, and the desire to prevent others from suffering a similar fate, is a great motivator when it comes to choosing a vocation.

As for me, the pain from my divorce caused me to contemplate a more satisfying, and, hopefully, impactful career than corporate HR. In this regard, I had an enormous amount of reference material. There was my experience with multiple therapists over a period of 15 years, the success I enjoyed with Al-Anon, and the invaluable guidance of my sponsor, Katie. Add to this the many self-help books I devoured, insights from well-known thinkers on self-development, such as Tony Robbins, and, of course, the wisdom of my always-supportive mother.

My formal education proved to be a solid foundation upon which I could build my new life. It's often said the most important thing you can acquire from traditional schooling is simply learning *how to learn.* Certainly, my education—particularly the degree I earned from USC—proved this. When you go to college, it's not necessarily the degree you receive in itself that's important, but rather the discipline and mental acuity you develop that stays with you into adulthood.

The structure and time allocated toward a degree of any stature is, in the end, more important than the supplemental certifications and training we receive along the way. In school, as in life, success is about mindset and how badly you want something. I longed to launch this new stage of my life just as intensely or more than I had wanted to earn my degree from 'SC. Now it was up to me to make it happen.

All of the puzzle pieces came together one afternoon in the fall of 2016. I was at home watching an interview with Tony Robbins. Everything he talked about, from raising one's standards, to changing one's mindset, completely resonated with me. The more he talked, the more I wanted to learn. So I went online, found his website and a page describing his life coach training programs and online content. Although intrigued, I didn't know enough about the program or its record of success to investigate much further. A few months later, however, on Thanksgiving Day, I received an email offering me one of Robbins' training programs. I applied immediately. I knew in my soul this was the path I was destined to take.

The quest for self-improvement played a big role in my decision to embark on this new career path. My divorce had left me realizing I desperately needed emotional and spiritual independence. I also required regular personal inventories to benchmark my progress and determine where I needed attention. As they teach us in Al-Anon, growth and developments are tasks we can never truly complete, but still, I knew intuitively it was time to go deeper, to find myself in ways I had never before.

Was I reticent? Reluctant? Skeptical? Not at all! In fact, I was more confident about this decision than I had been about any other in my entire life. The path ahead appeared clear and well-lit and I couldn't wait to get started.

Robbins' online life coach training program, accomplished through the Robbins-Madanes institute, took nine months to complete. How appropriate. This is about the same amount of time it takes to carry a baby to term. The program was as life changing as advertised...and more. As I've said, I had been acting as a coach in my corporate HR role, but this life-changing curriculum took me way beyond anything I had done before. The more I delved into the material, the more I felt like this was something I wanted to do with my life. No, this was something I *had* to do. Life coaching not only promised me direction, it promised *purpose*, something I desperately needed.

Still, even after completing Robbins' course and receiving my certificate, I didn't feel confident enough to formally hang out my professional shingle. I needed to prove to myself, if to no one else, that I could really offer something of value. So I contacted nearly a dozen people I knew from my network and offered to counsel them for free. *This would be my internship.* If it worked, I would provide them a valuable service. And if it didn't, well, I would not have robbed them of their hard-earned money. This "beta testing phase" was not without its challenges, but each proved to be a valuable learning experience. After carefully working with my volunteers for several months and recording the results, I felt confident enough to schedule my grand opening.

Setting Up Shop

No fly-by-night, seat-of-the-pants operation, my practice was a legitimate business complete with a

California state-issued business license, DBA, and business checking account. I created a business plan, set aside a budget, and designed a branding and marketing campaign to attract clients. This included traditional advertising as well as producing bite-size life coaching episodes for YouTube, called The MAK Show. And, of course, there was the most powerful tool of all: word-of-mouth marketing through my personal network.

My strategy relied on the marketing principles I had learned earning my business degree at USC, along with creating new branding strategies I believed would set me apart from my competition. Focused on offering something different, I tried to focus on traditionally underserved segments I felt could use support and help. For example, I founded a men's group targeting South Asian men.

Why this group? For one, being South Asian myself, I felt I could offer a strong emotional connection that people from other ethnic backgrounds might not. Next, because of my background, I knew too well how our culture grooms men to behave a certain way, express themselves in a certain way, and even feel a certain way. I also know how harshly judged men from this culture can be for stepping beyond strictly proscribed boundaries. Beyond personal experience, my research suggested these individuals have an especially hard time asking for help. As a result, having a trusting support system that can accept them unconditionally would prove to be key.

Developing the BRAVE System

As my life coaching practice grew, the principles I was using to address my clients' challenges began to coalesce into a formalized system that I ultimately decided to call BRAVE. There are several aspects of BRAVE I believe set it apart from virtually every other self-improvement program I have encountered. First, it's simple. BRAVE consists of just five elements: Beliefs>>>*Benevoliefs*, Readiness, Alignment, Vision, and Engagement. In life, simplicity is power. Think: The Golden Rule. The 10 Commandments. Buddhism's Four Nobel Truths. Instead of offering a daunting or complicated system, it provides something accessible.

Next, BRAVE is easy to remember. A mnemonic device, its very name helps users quickly recall the elements. If my experience as a life coach has taught me anything, it's that bravery is more easily acquired when its elements can be quickly and easily recalled when needed. Finally, the system actually works! The BRAVE approach has helped my clients overcome emotional barriers, conquer age-old fears, and find the success and happiness they seek. Once I had the BRAVE system perfected, tested, and verified, my next step was to formalize it in the form of a book. *This book.* Why write a book? It occurred to me from the start that as an individual practitioner, I would be limited to counseling a finite number of people. There are only so many hours in a day, so many days in a year, and so many years in a working lifetime. Also, by necessity, my practice was limited to Southern California, Orange County in particular.

Life coaching being what it is, I wondered if my influence and impact could extend beyond this limited geographic area. After all, I do not have the extraordinarily extroverted personality of a Tony Robbins, or the extensive medical background of Deepak Chopra. Further, I am not sure I can imagine building the kind of nationwide marketing network both of these individuals have created. (At least not yet ...)

The more I considered it, the more a book made sense. Writing one would push me out of my comfort zone, yet it was still something I could create with sufficient focus and effort. Writing a book—putting my ideas to paper, or more accurately, typing them—would help crystallize the concepts I had spent years devising. Finally, a book would be something that could impact hundreds, if not thousands of people. The more I thought about it, the more it became clear that this could be an effective vessel for transforming the lives of others. In short, a book was the ideal way to help more people get better. To make them BRAVE.

Now that you know a little bit more about how I *mindshifted* my own thinking to start what I view as my life's work, let's turn our focus to one of my clients who transcended her own challenges by going inward. Instead of trying to fix the world, together we worked on trying to fix *her* from the inside out.

Case Study: Shanti

Shanti is a 37-year-old Indian-American female. From an early age, she felt confused and fearful of what appeared to be a hostile world. However, due to our work together, she found her own bravery, allowing her to transcend a lifetime of depression and self-doubt, leading to self-actualization.

Like mine, Shanti's challenges began in childhood. Since she was young, she had suffered from clinical depression, social anxiety, and immense loneliness. This led her to practice various forms of self-harm, including cutting and promiscuity, as well to regularly entertain suicidal thoughts. Although she was an excellent student, her feelings of failure and rejection forced her to drop out of graduate school during her doctoral program.

State of Mind

The relatively faceless university environment in which Shanti found herself led to a loss of personal identity. Though she successfully earned her undergraduate degree, she developed intense anxiety about graduate school, experiencing an overwhelming fear of failure for the first time in her life. She also felt painfully alone.

Situation

Shanti's depression led to stress-eating, causing her to gain 70 pounds in one year. The combined weight gain and anxiety created a vicious circle of more self-loathing, more stress-eating, and more self-loathing. Worse, this resulted in her beginning to actively engage in self harming behaviors.

Status

While in the midst of her graduate studies, Shanti began to feel her life had become unmanageable. Unable to process her emotions, she dropped out of school. Intellectually, she knew this was a mistake, but could not find the courage to make herself return. Aware she could not find relief on her own, she turned to several sources for help, including me.

Being BRAVE

Beliefs >>> *Benevoliefs* (I am the Teacher and the Student):

Shanti believed she was not a worthy person and would fail as a student (both in school and life).

We replaced this with a new *benevolief*: Shanti is a lifelong learner who will experience a long, fulfilling and successful life.

Readiness (The Bell Rang):

Together, Shanti and I developed the habit of feeling and expressing gratitude, especially around her father, who had always supported her steadfastly. She is currently planning to write a book about her experience and plans to emphasize the gratitude she feels for those who stood by her during her emotional travails.

Together, we developed several personal affirmation statements to reinforce her new, positive thinking. This included the affirmation: "I have a beautiful spirit and I will work to showcase it on the outside in a healthy image."

We then translated these affirmations into action steps to better her life. Improving her physical health was a top priority. To do this, we adjusted her diet to include more nutritious foods, while also designing an easy-to-follow daily exercise regimen. To help her overcome her fear of higher education, I encouraged her to pursue her interest in art; not as an academic pursuit, but as a hobby. Once she realized she could find pleasure in such activities, her resistance to engaging in more formal, academic studies would likely diminish.

Engagement (Ready to Graduate):

Talk therapy has been proven to be even more effective than pharmaceuticals when it comes to dealing with depression. I therefore suggested Shanti meet with me several times per week. During these sessions, she was free to express and explore her feelings without fear of judgment.

We identified other tools Shanti could use to improve her mood and attitude, including daily exercise, and modified her schedule to prioritize rest and sleep, healthy food options, and other beneficial activities, such as reading.

Finally, we developed strategies she could use to make her interactions with family members less stressful. These included staging family meetings in which she would appear as her true herself.

Outcomes

After employing the BRAVE method for several months, Shanti reported strong positive results. For one, she recounted an increased sense of personal authenticity. She believed she had a better idea of who she really was and could now face life on her own terms. This, in turn, gave her a stronger sense of safety and security. She no longer felt threatened by the world and did not fear the judgment of others, especially her parents. As her sense of personal power increased, her incidents of self-harm diminished before finally stopping entirely.

I am happy to report she was able to return to grad school, free from the debilitating fears that had caused her to abandon her education earlier. Today, Shanti is happily married and the mother of two children. She is able to manage her emotional states and no longer fears the future. She completed her post-graduate studies and now holds a Ph.D. in education and runs a consulting firm in Los Angeles.

What I Learned from this Client

My work with Shanti taught me that many troubled people just need someone to talk to. They need empathy from a trusted confidant, someone who can listen without judging. I was also reminded recovery is an ongoing process that often occurs in fits and starts. There will always be stumbling blocks and setbacks, yes.

But setbacks are not failures, and we must learn to face adversity with a positive, can-do attitude, despite fears and self-doubts. After all, an unwavering belief in success can often become a self-fulfilling prophesy. It is often said the teacher learns most from his/her students and I am no exception. I took many of the lessons Shanti used to improve her life to manage my own uncertainties.

Quote:

"If you confirm your FEARS, self-reliance can be a confirmed belief in yourself."

For contemplation

Have you had to deal with mental illness in your life —perhaps your own or someone close to you? What did this experience take from you? What did it add?

Affirmation: *"Our mind is our guide, but we can influence it with our heart."*

Exercise:

It can be difficult to understand and accept a loved one's addiction, depression, or mental illness. This often leads to intense feelings of guilt. Even among family members where bonds are strong, addiction can lead us to suffer feelings of shame, disbelief, and confusion. In such circumstances, it is important we don't get trapped in a relationship of codependency. When dealing with an addict, one may feel compelled to take over and assume responsibility for the addict's behavior in the mistaken belief the addict is no longer—or at least temporarily—incapable of handling his/her own affairs. Instead, it is far better to do the following:

1. Offer support and understanding
2. Consider consulting professional help if needed.
3. Be honest about your concerns but remember to take care of yourself. You need to stay grounded and aligned to be helpful to your loved one.

Chapter 8
How Being BRAVE Changed My Life

As I detailed in previous chapters, I created the BRAVE system to help deal with my own personal pains and struggles. Growing up, I did not consider myself a strong person. I was a less-than-stellar student, an even less-accomplished athlete, and while I had a very large and loving family, I had only a small circle of friends that knew me well. As a member of a then-small ethnic minority, I was always curious as to how I could be more authentically me. Even though I dressed like my peers, listened to the same music, watched the same movies and TV shows, and spoke the same way as my schoolmates, my darker complexion banished me to the periphery of my social sphere.

As I've said, I was also not particularly good at meeting others' expectations. My parents, while loving and supportive, were also fairly strict and conservative. They had a very specific picture of the woman they wanted me to become, and I had neither the right tools nor the desire to live the life they desired. Consequently, as an adult, I spent a great deal of time in search of the right career.

Unlike many young people, it was not my dream to become rich and famous, or popular and powerful, or to create something so profound it would, in the words of the late Steve Jobs, "put a dent in the universe." My default ambition was to be a conventional wife and mother. Yet I also enjoyed working and contributing, being a strong partner and contributing to my family unity. This led me to enter a problematic marriage with a charismatic but ultimately self-destructive person who made me further question my own worth and potential. Among other things, one truly positive thing to come out of our long and difficult union was our daughter, whom I love dearly. Even so, the trauma of trying to raise a daughter in a dangerously unstable home led me to limit my maternal ambitions to having this single child.

After years of attempting to salvage a problematic marriage, I accepted the inevitability of divorce. I now had to learn to live with the shame and guilt I associated with this decision, while also navigating the practical difficulties of raising a child in two separate homes. Although I had frequently been something of a loner and was certainly not connected to my neighbors or the wider community, my separation from Umesh truly left me feeling more lonely, isolated, and powerless than ever. Something had to change.

The Beginning of a New Coping System

Ironically, ending my marriage gave me something I had had precious little of before: time. With this time, I was finally able to take a hard, objective took at myself. I used this opportunity to reassess and reevaluate my priorities, adjusting my perspective on what was truly important in life and what was not. At age 40, I realized my adventure on this Earth was now half over, and if I were going to accomplish something of value in my remaining years, I needed to devise a whole new game plan and get moving quickly. Most of all, I was going to have to find the will to see my new life plan through to completion.

Initially, realizing I had to start over filled me with dread. Getting through my youth had been difficult at times, but at least then I had the advantage of having the energy, vitality, and romantic view of the future that is the province of the young. When you're growing up, the future can seem strange and foreboding, but you don't yet know enough to understand how brutal life can be. There's a reason most mathematicians make their greatest breakthroughs while in their 20s, why most technical innovators and start-up entrepreneurs are barely out of school, and why most millionaires make their first million by age 30: They're all too young to know any better.

The BRAVE system was my roadmap out of despair and back into the world of possibilities. By changing my self-limiting BELIEFS into affirmative *BENEVOLIEFS*, I was able to *mindbreak* out of old, failed ways of thinking and *mindshift* myself into a state where I could accept new challenges and aim for greater heights.

Beliefs to Benevoliefs

To give you a sense of the importance of establishing *benevoliefs*, let's talk about the power of a positive mental attitude. In the first half of the 20th century, athletes throughout the world attempted, in vain, to run a four-minute mile. After failure after failure, physicians and researchers concluded running a mile in under four minutes was, for a human, a physical impossibility. The human body, they declared, just could not achieve the level of speed and endurance necessary to accomplish this feat.

And yet, on May 6, 1954, Englishman Roger Bannister ran four miles in three minutes and 59.4 seconds at Oxford University's Iffley Road track. In the following months, several other athletes matched and then smashed Bannister's historic record. To date, more than 1,400 athletes have run the four-minute mile.

So, what changed? Did human physiology suddenly take an evolutionary leap forward? Were advances in sports medicine able to suddenly create a whole generation of super runners? No, the only thing that changed was people's *belief* in a trained runner's ability to run a four-minute mile. For decades, everyone thought it was impossible, and as a result, no one was able to do it. But when a person—just one person—showed that it *could* be done—the world *mindshifted*, and the floodgates opened.

This is exactly what I have seen in both my personal life and my career as a life coach. The fact is, history is replete with challenges that "experts" insisted could never be overcome, from running the four-minute mile to climbing Mount Everest to creating a heavier-than-air flying machine to landing on the moon. While skill, effort, and determination are all essential components of success, it all starts with the belief that success is, in fact, achievable.

Readiness

By readying myself through exercise, education, and meditation, I was able to acquire the skills, resilience and, most importantly, the *confidence* necessary to set my life on its new path. They say success occurs when preparation meets opportunity. You can't always control the opportunities that present themselves—luck is, after all *luck*—random happenstance—but you *can* ready yourself to take maximum advantage of such opportunities when they occur.

For example, Broadway shows have cast members who serve as understudies for the lead roles; in the event that a star is sick, injured, or otherwise unable to perform, the understudy has to fill this role, often at a moment's notice. Many understudies train for months, but never get a chance to play the lead. And then there are stories about actors—such as Shirley MacLaine, Sutton Foster, Bernadette Peters and Matthew Morrison—who, after slaving away as unrecognized understudies, were one night tapped to fill in for a waylaid lead. Because they were prepared, were able to wow audiences and launch themselves to stardom. When I set off on the BRAVE program, I recognized I, too, was readying myself to take advantage of opportunities that might never come. But if they *did* come, damn it if I wasn't going to be ready!

Alignment

If you own a car, you know that if your front wheels are out of alignment—even slightly—your vehicle can become difficult to handle, not to mention it can significantly shorten your tires' lifespan. Likewise, a laser's extreme power is due to its light rays being intensely aligned in a single direction. In physics, this is called *coherence*. And we've all heard the expression, "difficult as herding cats," illustrating the frustrations that occur when parts of a system—be it an organization, or a single individual—go wandering off in different directions.

When it came to realigning my own actions with my new goals, I was able to make progress as efficiently as possible under the BRAVE system. To my great surprise, I was able to minimize costly distractions while steering clear of avoidable obstacles in this new stage. I can't emphasize enough how important it is to ensure all aspects of your life not only support each other, but also point in the same direction. Aligning your work life with your home life, your home life with your personal life, and your personal life with your spiritual life, can be difficult. But if you can achieve such alignment, life in general becomes *significantly* easier.

Trust me. I know this, firsthand.

Vision

During this period, I developed an idea of what I wanted my life to become. This was not just some vague aspiration, like "be happier" or "make more money," but rather a specific, detailed image of the person I wanted to be and the life I wanted to live. At this point, I wish to specifically differentiate "vision" from the "Law of Attraction" as promoted by authors such as Rhonda Byrne in her 2006 best-seller, *The Secret*.

The so-called Law of Attraction not only posits that negative thoughts and positive thoughts can lead to corresponding outcomes, but also that thinking hard enough about something can actually make it occur. I do strongly believe that how we think governs how we behave. If we believe we are going to fail in a specific task, we are far more likely be discouraged by even minor setbacks and less likely to put in the additional effort that may be necessary to achieve a positive outcome. Belief in impending failure, or pessimism, can all too often become a self-fulfilling prophecy. Conversely, if we believe we are destined for success, we are less likely to allow setbacks to stall our forward momentum, allowing us to persevere through even difficult phases of our life's journey. In other words, positive thinking doesn't *guarantee* success, but it does make it more likely.

Despite what some people would prefer, you can't just think about a new car and get a new car, or just think about conquering cancer and then wake up cancer free. The universe doesn't work that way. Notwithstanding what you might have heard about quantum mechanics and mind/body interaction, the idea that you can manifest your own reality is just another example of what some call "magical thinking," and it is not part of the BRAVE philosophy. Instead, I coach my clients to do the inner work, to get right with themselves so they can improve in all of the facets of their lives.

Engagement

Finally, I made *results* my top priority, putting my self-improvement plan into action. This was perhaps the most difficult part of the entire process. Relatively speaking, planning is easy. It's also fun. There is great pleasure in imagining life's possibilities. (Who hasn't imagined what they'd do if they won the lottery?) However, actually putting a plan into action—then dealing with the outcomes—can be both frightening to contemplate and hard to do in practice.

As the great Prussian field marshal Helmuth von Moltke so famously stated, "No plan survives first contact with the enemy." No matter how fervent your beliefs, how strong your motivation, how thorough your preparation, and how clear your vision, once you start moving, you're going to encounter obstacles and snags you never saw coming. This is where perseverance, flexibility, and improvisation come into play. People who succeed are able to think on their feet, roll with the punches, and forge ahead without ever taking their eyes of the prize. The ability to thoroughly engage grows out of an unwavering belief in the value of one's goals and the confidence in one's self to achieve them. (Which is what I developed the longer I employed the BRAVE system.)

What Changed in Me

It may sound easy to suggest the above to others. After all, anyone can offer advice. The real test is seeing something through to the end.

So, did I do the work myself to prove BRAVE does what it promises? I'm happy to say I did. And it does. Unequivocally. In just my first year of being BRAVE, my life completely transformed for the better in many ways. These changes weren't just emotional or cosmetic; they were specific and measurable. They included:

Confidence

For virtually all of my adult life, Umesh managed much of my financial affairs. Now that he was no longer a part of my day-to-day life, I had to create my own household budget, pay my bills, and manage my savings. Initially, the prospect of this new responsibility terrified me. Yet by adhering to the tenets I established when creating BRAVE, I developed the confidence necessary to handle this most fundamental of tasks.

After a few months, I was no longer fearful about money or my ability to handle it. I became confident enough to make some small but still impactful high-yielding investments. Even more importantly, I legally incorporated and focused on growing my business. Within a year my income rose 150 percent. For the first time in my life, I was no longer living paycheck to paycheck. It was a wonderful feeling. In this society, money is power. Money is freedom. And only by understanding and controlling money can we be truly liberated as individuals. Through acting BRAVE in this regard, I was able to gain more financial independence, increasing my confidence to handle life's challenges.

Emotional Control

As I described earlier, for years, much of my day-to-day existence had felt like an emotional roller coaster: euphoric highs followed by depressing downs. Though I was not clinically bipolar, I nonetheless had trouble controlling my moods, which tended to whipsaw between anger, sadness, joy, and terror.

It's sad to say, but I sometimes felt like the poster child for introversion; fearful around other people and only truly comfortable in solitude. But after practicing the principles of BRAVE—particularly daily meditation—I found I could not only function comfortably in the company of others, but also actually thrive in the experience.

Actors and stand-up comics often talk about how they feed off the energy of their audiences, that being the center of attention can be like nourishment for the spirit. As a life coach with a growing set of clients who began going on podcasts and radio shows, and speaking to groups, I began to understand the adrenalin high you can receive from talking to crowds.

Likewise, after decades of social avoidance, I found more comfort and joy in the company of others. My moods became more stable, my general outlook increasingly positive. Sure, bad news still upset me, but it no longer crushed me. Setbacks still annoyed me, but they no longer sent me into fits of rage or recriminations. For the first time in my life, I finally believed I understood what "normal" felt like.

Health

They say when you have your health, you have everything. I don't know that this is literally true, but there's no doubt that the *lack* of health makes it impossible to enjoy life's pleasures. All of us have been sick at some points in our lives—everything from miserable head colds to debilitating viruses. Some of us have also had to deal with the horrors of cancer, diabetes, strokes, AIDS, and other life-threatening diseases. Unfortunately, too many of us rely on modern medicine to provide cures for when our bodies fail us when the fact is we do far too little to keep our bodies from failing in the first place.

It's true that Western medicine has really delivered when it comes to preventing and curing a whole host of afflictions. At the same time, vaccines have rid humanity of such scourges as smallpox and polio and have all but eliminated communicable childhood diseases such as measles, chicken pox, diphtheria, and whooping cough. Modern medical devices and pharmaceuticals have allowed people with all manner of formerly debilitating and potentially fatal conditions to live longer, happier lives. But an overreliance on medical science and technology has caused too many of us to ignore the simple lifestyle changes that can help us feel better, avoid disease, and recover from illness more quickly. I speak from personal experience because I was one of these people and turned my life around.

Never Say Diet

Before creating the BRAVE program, I lived like many 21st century middle-class Americans do. I ate too much. I exercised too little. My diet consisted of far too many convenience foods, including fast, frozen, and processed. I had an erratic sleep schedule, often getting fewer than six hours of sleep during the work week and then trying to catch up on the weekends.

I also felt under constant pressure to make every waking hour count, cramming my days full of as many obligations and tasks as I could handle, with precious little time for pure relaxation. As a result of these habits, I spent too much time feeling listless, anxious, irritable, and depressed. Thanks to the advice I received from my therapists, I came to understand that my behavior—not germs, not the environment—was at the root of most of these afflictions. According to my doctor, my poor eating habits not only accounted for my weight issues, but also had made me "pre-diabetic." He recommended that I lose 10 pounds as soon as possible as well as begin a regimen of medications designed to control my blood sugar.

As I mentioned earlier, I changed my diet after splitting up with Umesh. I replaced fast and processed foods with fresh, organic grains, fruits, and vegetables. I all but cut my intake of sugar and white bread down by 50 percent. (This was, without a doubt, the hardest part of my new diet!) As I came to learn, sugars easily become body fat, which in turn has been linked to higher risks of heart disease, diabetes, cancer, and stroke. Instead of eating on the run, I scheduled specific times for breakfast, lunch, and dinner. When it came to between meal and late-night snacking, I replaced candy, chips, and ice cream with berries, apples, nuts, granola, and air-popped popcorn. I stopped eating milk and other dairy products altogether.

The transition from junk to healthy foods was easier than I had anticipated. Most of the healthy foods described above are easy to prepare in any number of delicious ways. Dining out is no problem, since virtually all restaurants—

even fast food ones—offer healthy options on their menus. As for avoiding sugar and white bread, it's really all about being mindful.

In other words, *paying attention.*

When you're out and tempted to grab a candy bar or an ice cream cone, stop and ask yourself, "Is this going to help me or hurt me?" Perhaps most important of all, don't look at your new eating style as a "diet"—which most people think of as temporary —or as a prohibition. (If the 1920s taught as anything, it's that prohibitions don't work. Especially when they involve things people really, really like.) Yes, you can still eat ice cream. Just less of it and less often. Yes, you can still have a piece of cake. But just on special occasions. Soon, your new, good eating habits will replace your old, bad ones, and each day will be easier than the one before it. I now know this from personal experience!

Sweet Dreams

Sleep, and its purpose, has long been a mystery for humankind. While dreams have, for centuries, played a major role in religion, poetry, and drama, and are believed to be linked to everything from prophesy to visits by spirits of the dead, their origins and meanings have never been truly explained. In the late 19th century, Dr. Sigmund Freud, the father of modern psychoanalysis, believed dreams were a gateway to the human subconscious and, by studying them, one could find the root of neuroses, phobias, and other mental afflictions. In the 20th and 21st centuries, researchers spent countless hours studying the biological, physical, and chemical nature of sleep and of dreams, and have yet to find a definitive answer to their function.

There are a few things we know for sure. Sleep is critical to life. All creatures, from the lowliest insects to the most complex mammals, sleep in one form or another. In humans, sleep is particularly critical to both our physical and mental health. Sleep is necessary to recharge the immune system, heal wounds, and regulate weight. Sleep is also critical to proper mental and memory functions. Without prolonged deep, and regular sleep, we quickly lose our ability to concentrate and to properly process information. Our reaction time slows. Our ability to form long-term memories falters. We lose physical dexterity and coordination. Sleep deprivation is also linked emotional instability, weight gain, and even violence.

As I mentioned earlier, after recovering from my divorce, I made sure to make adopting good sleeping habits a priority. Instead of pushing myself to stay awake as long as possible, I made sure to get at least seven hours every night. I started going to bed and getting up at the same time every day, even on weekends. I discovered having a set bedtime every day helped me fall asleep faster, sleep harder, and wake up with less effort. I still enjoyed my morning cup of coffee, but if I had to do without it, it wasn't the end of the world.

As a result of these improvements, my overall health improved markedly. My colds became less and less frequent. When I did get sick, I recovered in just days rather than weeks. In my 20s and 30s, I got cold sores on my lips whenever my immunity weakened, which happened about three or four times a year. Now, they rarely appear at all.

Improving from the inside out physically had tremendous positive effects on me outwardly. Not only did I begin to feel better, the world opened up to me in wonderful new ways—which is exactly the kind of thinking and doing I counsel my clients.

A Word about Alcohol

As I just described, my early experiences with alcohol were fairly typical of people of my generation. In high school and college, alcohol was a fixture of virtually every party and social gathering, and it was all but impossible to have a social life without imbibing. Drinking also played a big role in bringing Umesh and me together. As I've frequently noted, he was a "party boy," someone who became more fun and gregarious the more alcohol he consumed. As a young woman, I found this behavior attractive and, being eager to have as much fun as possible, was more than happy to try keeping up.

But after we married and Umesh's hard-drinking ways continued, I became less and less enamored with this lifestyle. Terrified by the changes I saw in Umesh's personality when he drank, as well as the damage he was doing to our relationship and our finances, I finally gave up drinking altogether.

After our daughter was born, I swore never to touch alcohol again. I was terrified that any drinking would endanger her well-being, and I would never be able to live with the guilt. Even after I divorced Umesh, I took great pains to avoid contact with alcohol—if for no other reason than to support his efforts to achieve sobriety. I certainly didn't want my daughter to be exposed to anything like that again.

It was only through my work with Al-Anon that I finally worked my way past my aversion to alcohol and was able to again enjoy the occasional "adult beverage" without experiencing feelings of guilt and remorse. At Al-Anon, I learned that alcoholism, while a disease, is not communicable. In this sense, it is more like cancer or Alzheimer's than it is AIDS or influenza. And while an alcoholic's only sure recourse is to avoid alcohol for the rest of their life, this is not the case for non-alcoholic family members. If we can be satisfied with just a drink or two and comfortably avoid the temptation to drink to excess, we should feel perfectly free to do so. As for my aversion to drinking, I came to understand that my reaction was to the negative behaviors I associated with alcohol—not to the alcohol itself. For me, this was a major breakthrough.

With the *mindshift* I experienced as a result of developing the BRAVE program, I was able to find the courage to attempt a return to social drinking. After 16 years of sobriety, the transition was not without its difficulties. But with practice, support, and recognizing I had no one pressuring me one way or the other, I found I could once again drink at parties, enjoy a cocktail at dinner, or end the workweek with a glass of wine without having my world collapse around me. I was like a soldier finally able to deal with the trauma of PTSs and again function in the normal world.

On Guilt

There is a great amount of guilt that comes with divorce. Even though divorce is far more common today than it was a few generations ago, no one goes through the experience emotionally unscathed. Many people see divorce as a form of death, and I suppose I can understand this feeling. It is the death of a relationship. The death of a possible future. And certainty the death of one's belief in happily ever after.

After my divorce, I felt a little like Hester Prynne in *The Scarlet Letter*, only instead of walking around with a big red "A" on my chest, it was a big flashing "D."

Amazingly, I was the only member of my small social circle to have endured this trauma, and I felt like the elephant in the room whenever we would get together. As a result, I withdrew socially, not wanting to expose them to my shame. Fortunately, several of them proactively made attempts to contact and console me. I suppose this was the test that showed who my real friends were.

As with my return to social drinking, it took me several months and a lot of hard work to overcome the guilt associated with my divorce. Thanks to the BRAVE program, I was eventually able to come to a better understanding of who I was, what I was capable of, and why my divorce from Umesh was not only necessary, but also desirable. I was able to view it as the empowering, liberating experience that it was. There was no need to feel guilty. No reason to feel shame. I was now standing on my own two feet, and for that I should feel nothing but pride.

Below, please find the case studies of one of my clients who was also facing seemingly insurmountable challenges before going within and transforming himself through the BRAVE approach.

Case Study: Rob

Rob, a Caucasian male, was 60 years old when I began working with him. Having served in law enforcement for 25 years, he was due to retire from the force, but didn't want to quit working. Instead, he wished to move into the private sector, specifically corporate security. The problem was, he wasn't sure if his skills would transfer easily, or if there would even be a job available for someone his age. Like my own feelings of ineptitude following my divorce, these doubts led Rob to experience overall self-confidence issues.

State of Mind

Rob had a specific goal: to land a job in corporate security management. However, a self-defeating mistrust of his own abilities and available opportunities caused him to defer seeking new employment.

Situation

Rob had not yet developed any job search strategies. He knew he desired a new career but had no idea how to affect lasting positive change in his life.

Status

To prepare Rob for his job search, I coached him on interview strategies and techniques, helping to package his previous law enforcement experience in language better suited to today's corporate environment. When it came to developing his resume and interviewing skills, we focused on making him "solution-oriented," the type of person who could help companies solve their internal and external security problems.

Being BRAVE

Beliefs >>> *Benevoliefs:* (Get Right on the Inside):

Rob was impaired by his belief that he was too old and not connected enough with key decision makers to transfer his law enforcement skills to corporate security. We replaced this limiting thinking with the *benevolief* that he possessed valuable, highly marketable skills immediately applicable in this new field, and that he could handle all the steps necessary to make the transition.

Readiness (Going Within):

Rob believed he was not prepared for the process of securing a new job, so we outlined the following steps to *mindshift:*

Work together to strategically plan for his upcoming job search.

Adjust to a problem-solving mentality. Together, we honed in on what problems prospective employers were likely experiencing, and what solutions, general or specific, Rob could provide (based on his considerable experience level, not his age). I wanted Rob to see himself as a "go-to guy" for solving corporate security challenges and not some out of touch has-been.

Enhance Rob's people-management skills. Drawing examples from his experiences in law enforcement, I encouraged him to educate himself on leadership philosophies, skills, and techniques so he would be confident he would bring a wealth of value to any new organization.

Alignment (Connecting past to present):

We positioned Rob as an expert who offers strategic solutions, packaging his law enforcement history to suit a corporate environment, and preparing him to assume a service mindset. (Something previously beyond his comfort zone.)

Vision (It's Never Too Late to Be Great):

Together, Rob and I created a vision statement reflecting the person he wanted prospective employers to see. He envisioned himself engaging in work about which he felt passionate, in becoming a thought leader to whom others turned to for advice, insight, and solutions.

Engagement (Ready for Primetime):

We used talk therapy to help Rob build his self-confidence, changing his internal conversations from positive to negative. We also engaged in mock interviews so he could mentally prepare himself to answer the kind of questions he would likely encounter.

Outcomes (Transcending Expectations)

Rob went on more than a half dozen interviews, has had several call-backs, and ultimately was offered a director role with a large organization in Peoria, Arizona. His success was due, in no small part, to his improved self-confidence. His continued progress has only provided additional positive reinforcement. He now has a much better perspective of his value in the professional marketplace as well as renewed confidence in his self-worth.

What I Learned from This Client

My work with Rob once again reminded me of the value of perseverance and determination. Also, I saw again how a *mindbreak* out of old, destructive habits and a *mindshift* into new, positive modes of thinking can provide us with a truer perspective of ourselves and the opportunities the world offers us. I needed to find my self-confidence to recover from the trauma of my divorce, just as Rob needed to find his to transition from the public sector to private enterprise.

Quote:

Take the anxiety out of your performance by telling yourself, "I'm eager and ready!"

For contemplation:

What about yourself makes you feel most confident? In what area do you most need confidence to succeed?

Affirmation:

"I exercise my strengths and my weaknesses. I am friendly, open, and confident with other people."

Exercise:

Speak to three new people, giving them genuine compliments so as to build up their self-worth (and in the process, your own.)

Chapter 9
Your Turn to Be BRAVE

Over the past eight chapters, I've taken you on an abbreviated tour of my life as an Indian-American woman, student, wife, mother, divorcee, corporate HR officer, and life coach. I've described the challenges I've faced along the way—challenges rooted in fear, self-doubt, feelings of inadequacy, and codependency—and showed how, for decades, I felt less than brave.

Throughout these pages, I discussed the major influences in my later life—most notably Al-Anon and author, philanthropist, and life coach Tony Robbins—and how, over time, I combined the wisdom received with my own experiences to create BRAVE. Drawing upon these five simple steps: B)ELIEF>>*BENEVOLIEF*, (R)EADINESS, (A)LIGNMENT, (V)ISION, and (E)NGAGEMENT, I believe anyone can find the needed courage to *mindbreak* from old, destructive habits, and *mindshift* to a new personal reality bringing success and happiness.

So now it's time to put these principles to work in *your* life. It's time to take the ideas I've presented and apply them to your own challenges, whether they be personal or professional. It's time to overcome fears, vanquish doubts, and silence insecurities. Now is the moment to seize opportunities, achieve astonishing victories, and find true peace and contentment. We are ready to declare, "This life is mine, and I'm going to make the most of it."

In short, it's time to be BRAVE.

Setting Goals

When constructing a story, it's important the author give the hero a specific goal to pursue. Goals provide narratives with a sense of purpose and direction. Once the hero has a goal, the audience becomes eager to go along for the ride, to see if and how the hero will achieve their goal. In *The Wizard of Oz*, Dorothy wants to go home. In George Lucas's *Star Wars,* Luke Skywalker wants to deliver R2-D2 to Alderaan (and later destroy the Death Star). In James Cameron's *Titanic*, Rose wants to escape an arranged marriage to a rich but abusive brute and pursue a free, fulfilling life with Jack. Not every character achieves their goal, yet what they experience in the attempt is what gives stories their impact and meaning. Without a goal, stories tend to be meandering and uninspiring.

In real life, just as in fiction, it's important to have goals. Goals give our life direction. They offer purpose—a reason to wake up in the morning, as well as milestones against which we can judge our progress. Similar to the heroes of movies and novels, we may not always achieve our goals, but what we learn along the way inevitably makes our lives richer, deeper, and more profound.

When engaging the BRAVE system, the first step is to set a goal. This may not be as easy as you think. A viable goal needs to be specific. It needs to be attainable. And it needs to be framed in terms of time. For example, it's not enough to simply say, "I want to be rich," "I want to be an artist," or "I want to be happy." These are ambitions, not goals. *What's the difference?* An ambition is broad, long-term. It describes an ongoing state you not only want to achieve, but also *maintain.* It you want to be rich, one assumes you want to *stay* rich. If you want to be an artist, one assumes you want to make a long-term career out of it. If you want to be happy, one assumes you want to *remain* happy for the rest of your life.

Goals, on the other hand, are short-term, finite. A good example is the literal goal of scoring in soccer. You achieve this by kicking the ball past the goalie and into the net. Once this goal is achieved, you score a point. But the game isn't over. It continues until the clock runs out. Until it does, each team has more goals to score. (And more goals to *prevent* the opposing team from scoring.) By the way, a goal can just as easily involve *stopping* something from happening as well as achieving a positive objective. For instance, the movie *Speed* is all about a hero trying to stop a bomb from blowing up a speeding bus.

So what is *your* immediate goal? To lose 10 pounds? To buy a new car? To get married? To get a new job or earn a valuable promotion? When contemplating goal setting, think of something specific. The more specific the better. (But don't get hung up on details. If your goal is to buy a new car, you don't have to state the specific make and model. You may find a better deal on a wholly different vehicle while looking!)

Next, give yourself a deadline. Deadlines are important. They put pressure on your to actually *get the job done.* When do you want to lose those 10 pounds? By the end of the month? In two months? By your birthday? Make your deadline tight but realistic. Be ambitious, but don't set yourself up for failure. Above all, make the goal something you really want. Something you find important. Something you believe will improve your life and is worth fighting to achieve. Something for which you are willing to sacrifice. The more important the goal, the more you will be willing to fight to achieve it. (And the less likely you'll be to abandon it when the going gets tough.)

Turning a Belief into a *Benevolief*

Now that you have chosen a goal, it's time to ask yourself: Why have I not achieved this earlier? What has been keeping me from having this sooner? Chances are, you hold a belief that has deterred you from pursing your objective. For example, if you want to lose 10 pounds, you may believe dieting will be arduous and frustrating. You'll have to give up all the foods you enjoy. You'll become weak and irritable. You may also believe that even if you do manage to lose your intended weight, you won't be able to keep it off for long.

Likewise, if you want to buy a new car, you may hold similar limiting beliefs. You may be concerned it will be too expensive. You may think you won't qualify for the loan. Along the same lines, if you want to get married, you may believe you're unattractive and that no one will want to marry you. You may have a fear of commitment, of losing your freedom and independence. You might even believe the institution itself is fatally flawed, and that any marriage you enter into will likely end in a painful divorce. Last, if you want a new job or promotion, you may believe you won't measure up to an employer's standards, that your skills aren't competitive, that you're too young, too old, or that you won't be able to handle the new responsibilities.

Whatever your goal, begin identifying beliefs that have been holding you back. Ask yourself, what about these beliefs must you change to make you feel happier, healthier, and more fulfilled? What frightens you about changing your beliefs? What possibilities of change excites you most? Most of all, how can you transform your existing beliefs to serve you better, to become *benevoliefs*?

Exercise: Belief to *Benevolief*

Think again about your goal. Now contemplate the beliefs associated with this goal that have prevented you from pursing it. How did you come to possess these beliefs? How long have you held onto them, and why? To transcend what's kept you from achieving what you want, you need to take proactive measures. Begin to keep a journal in which you write down as much as you can about your beliefs and how they have influenced your life.

Turn to a new page and list the belief, reflecting what you need in your life. (This is not about just flipping the belief 180 degrees—turning "can't" to "can"—instead, it's about describing in positive terms how your objective can be achieved.) Feel free to change or rephrase your belief any way you like until you have an affirmative statement that supports, rather than hinders, the goal you are trying to attain.

For example, again, if you want to lose 10 pounds and in the past believed dieting might be too difficult, the way to change this belief to a *benevolief* is to write something akin to the following: "I believe my diet is something I can control, that I can lose weight and avoid hunger by eating healthy, nutritious foods in moderate portions."

Let's return to some of the other examples. If you wish to buy a car but suspect you can't afford one or won't qualify for a loan, here is how you might structure your new *benevolief*: "I believe I can obtain a new vehicle—new or pre-owned—that fits my needs and my budget." If you want to get married but worry you will never find a partner, you can change this to a *benevolief* by writing something like: "I believe I am worthy of love. I believe there is someone I can make happy, and with whom I can find happiness." And if you want a new job or promotion but don't believe you have what it takes, change this to a *benevolief* like: "I believe my talent, training, experience, skills, attitude, and personality can be of great benefit to the [name of organization.]"

Quick caveat: the above is not "wishful thinking." It is about looking at a challenge from a positive, rather than a negative, perspective. Every day, people lose weight, buy cars, get married, land jobs, and do hundreds of other difficult things. The only difference between them and those who don't can be as simple as the fact the latter group has convinced themselves to not even *try*. They let fear and pessimism hold them back. As the saying goes, the only way to win the game is to play the game. And nobody plays well if they believe they're going to lose.

*****

Affirmation:

"I look forward to the changes that are coming next."

Readiness

Preparation is the key to success. The more difficult the challenge, the longer and more intense your preparation must be. Consider this: Doctors spend hundreds of hours learning human anatomy, chemistry, biology, and surgical techniques before ever meeting their first patients. They undergo intensive training before being handed their first scalpel.

Part of this preparation involves dissecting human corpses and practicing drawing blood from fellow students. Dealing with the grisly reality of anatomy, it's not unusual for fledgling students to become nauseated, panic, or even faint during such procedures. Only through repeated practice can some would-be doctors become desensitized to the overwhelming sights, smells, and sensations associated with medicine. Yet, over time, most do.

Like doctors, members of the armed forces must face dangers and traumatic situations most civilians will never face in their lifetimes. To prepare for combat, soldiers must not only optimize their physical performance and train on a variety of weapons, they must also desensitize themselves to sights and sounds that might send the untrained heading for the hills. For example, in basic training, it's common for soldiers to crawl through a barbed-wired-laden obstacle course while bullets fly within inches of their heads. Troops training for duty in the Middle East will first spend weeks in the American Southwest acclimating themselves to the brutal heat they'll have to endure while overseas. Mentally, they're training to shed their individuality, to see themselves as a part of a larger unit, a team with power and purpose bigger than themselves. To get there, they must learn to follow orders without question or analysis, something many find difficult to do. And, of course, service people traveling to distant, exotic locations have to inoculate themselves against diseases they are likely to be exposed to while serving abroad.

Stage actors undergo a different, but intensive, preparation for new roles. They usually rehearse for weeks—even months—before setting foot in front of an audience. Along the same lines, professional athletes must spend hours training for every minute they spend in actual play. Even the most celebrated professional musicians have to practice continuously to maintain their superior level of performance. As the late concert violinist Jascha Heifetz famously said, "If I don't practice one day, I know it; two days, the critics know it; three days, the public knows it."

So, what will it take for you to be ready?

Well, if you want to lose 10 pounds, after declaring your new *benevolief*, it's advisable to read up on the latest diet research, rid your house of tempting junk foods, and stock your kitchen with healthy, nutritious, low-calorie fare. You may even wish to consult with a professional nutritionist who can create a weekly meal plan that makes sense for your body type, lifestyle, and budget.

Now, if you want to buy a new car, it's a good idea to check online for expert recommendations on new and used vehicles. You also might want to take a comprehensive look at your monthly expenses to see where you can save money to put toward your new purchase. Also consider leasing as an option, instead of outright purchase. Check your credit score and make sure the reporting is accurate. Take steps to remove any inaccuracies that might be impeding your credit rating. Finally, you probably want to keep your eye out for sales and special promotions on vehicles in your general price range.

Onto finding that special someone. If you want to get married, you first have to determine *why* you want to get married. What kind of marriage do you want to create? Do you want a "traditional" marriage in which the husband works and the wife stays home and raises the kids? Or do you want a more modern marriage in which both spouses work and young children are raised by nannies or in daycare? Next, consider your values. When it comes to religious, political, and personal views, what are you looking for in a life partner? *Where* do you want to live? In what kind of community? In the city? In the suburbs? In a small town or are on a farm? In what kind of home? Single-family? Apartment? Do you want children? How many do you want and at what point in your life do you want to start a family? Other questions to consider: Who's going to handle the finances? Will you share a joint bank account? Might you want to get a prenuptial agreement? Why or why not?

Conflicts surrounding any of the above topics can strain even the seemingly happiest of marriages, so it's best to truly know *yourself* before looking for a partner. Last, if you want to get a new job or promotion, getting ready might involve researching a job or position to better understand how you might add value, taking an inventory of your skills, training, and accomplishments, adjusting your resume to best reflect your desired position, networking with friends, relatives, and associates to identify job openings, acquiring the right attire for interviews, and identifying which job hunting services are most likely to pair you with quality employers.

Bottom line: whether it be losing weight, buying a new car, finding that special someone, or landing your dream job, preparation is key. Once you've set the stage to be successful for whatever is you seek, you will be ready—and most important of all, you will *feel* ready—to hit the ground running.

Contemplation:

"What will it take for you to be ready?"

Exercise:

Make a checklist of five things you can do to prepare yourself now to pursue your goal. Attach a deadline for each activity.

*****

Affirmation:

"I am eager and ready to live a purposeful life."

Alignment

As stated earlier, alignment is the process of making sure the various aspects of your life are pointed in the direction you want to move. This includes your own attitudes, desires, and assumptions. In other words, it's about achieving focus.

Over the past few years, the ability to "multitask" has been celebrated throughout Western culture. Anyone who can prepare a home-cooked meal while attending to three unruly kids and preparing a PowerPoint presentation for the next day's investors' meeting is viewed as the epitome of the modern man or woman. There's just one problem with this model: It's a fake. A fabrication. A lie. At least according to several studies in which it has been argued that multitasking is mentally impossible. However, let's face it, there are times when we are forced to multitask. In these instances, exercising mindfulness to align with the most critical priorities must be reaffirmed to successfully execute what's needed.

Countless studies have shown multitasking to be mentally impossible. The human brain is hardwired through eons of biological evolution to concentrate on just one task at a time. A hundred thousand years ago, a *homo sapien* who wanted to make fire had to focus all of her energies on *making fire.* Concerns about the meat she wished to cook or the flint arrow tips she needed to sharpen would have to wait.

Likewise, a thousand years ago, a knight preparing to engage in battle had to focus on the fit of his armor, the position of his sword, and the behavior of his steed. If he let his mind wander to the roof back home needing thatching or how he might pay this month's royal taxes, such distractions might lead to a lance through his chest.

Today, a teenager who attempts to text or surf the web while driving a car is setting himself up for a metal-shredding, glass-shattering accident that could leave him permanently debilitated—or worse.

The truth is, we live in a hyperactive world. Stimulus overload is one of the reasons we're so unhappy and unfulfilled. Does it ever feel like half the time you're doing something you can't help but experience the nagging suspicion you should be using this moment for something else? And even when you do that "something else," you still can't help worrying about a half-dozen other tasks still pending? Regretfully, trying to accomplish 10 things at once doesn't lead to greater productivity. It leads poorer results in all 10 tasks.

In meditation, we are taught to clear the mind of thoughts; to become aware of only the here and now. For many, this can be one of the most difficult challenges we ever face. Ever since childhood, we've been encouraged to make the most of every moment, to not waste time, to live every day as if it were our last (YOLO!) Such conditioning makes the simple act of just *being*—allowing time to stream by unacknowledged and unaccounted for—feel uncomfortable, if not downright agonizing. Antithetical to the requirements of modern life, meditation can feel so unnerving at first that a lot of people can't handle it.

However, with just a little practice, meditation can offer a salve for the modern era. Clearing our minds of everything but the task at hand can not only be liberating, but also empowering. Think of your mental components— your desire, your motivation, your skill set—like the wheels on a car or the engines on an airplane. They must all point in the same direction or they won't go anywhere. Similarly, when all your energies are directed at a single goal, you'll advance faster and with less resistance than you might have thought possible.

Let's put this notion in practice by returning to the examples of typical desires covered earlier. If you want to lose 10 pounds, you should be eating healthy, nutritious, unprocessed foods, not thinking about how much you're going to miss ice cream, fried chicken, and cheesecake. If you want to buy a new car, you should be budgeting for the necessary down payment and/or monthly payments, not spending your discretionary funds on high-end restaurants, new clothes, or entertainment. If you want to get married, you should be out meeting other single people, not obsessing over your career or binge-watching Netflix. And if you want a new job or promotion, you should be honing your professional skills, polishing your resume, and networking with professionals in your field, not doing chores or catching up on Facebook.

Yes, all of these other mentioned activities can, in fact, provide certain and perhaps even valuable benefits, but they won't take you where you want to go. Anything valuable requires sacrifice and effort to achieve. And the fact is, we must often forgo short-term pleasures to achieve long-term fulfillment.

Contemplation: What is the best possible outcome for your particular situation, and what is the most direct route for getting there?

Exercise: Engage in creative visualization to model the best possible outcome for your goal. Use magazine clippings or print pictures off the Internet to create a "vision board" illustrating what accomplishing your goal will feel like. This will help provide the needed motivation to push past obstacles and align yourself with success.

*****

Affirmation:

"I effortlessly reach my goals, small and large."

Vision

Business organizations, both for-profit and nonprofit, often develop a vision statement as part of their business plan. This is different from a mission statement that focuses on what a company is doing in the here and now. A vision statement instead describes what an organization hopes to accomplish long term. Here are some vision statement examples from well-known companies illustrating the power of forward thinking.

Tesla:
"To create the most compelling car company of the 21st century by driving the world's transition to electric vehicles."

Amazon:
"To be the Earth's most customer-centric company where customers can find and discover anything they might want to buy online."

Caterpillar:
"Our vision is a world in which all people's basic needs—such as shelter, clean water, sanitation, food and reliable power—are fulfilled in an environmentally sustainable way by a company that improves the quality of the environment and the communities where we live and work."

Uber:
"Smarter transportation with fewer cars and greater access. Transportation that's safer, cheaper, and more reliable; transportation that creates more job opportunities and higher incomes for drivers."

Southwest:

"To become the world's most loved, most flown, and most profitable airline."

*****

Though some of these vision statements are very broad (e.g. Caterpillar), and others very specific (e.g. Tesla, Southwest), what they share in common is they're future-focused. They're aspirational. They describe what the founders sought out to eventually accomplish and how they wished to be perceived.

As individuals, we also need vision statements. It's helpful to describe in brief, broad strokes the person we want to be and how we want others to view us. Creating such a statement goes hand-in-hand with goal setting but also transcends such activities. Broader and longer-term, visions can help shape attitudes, beliefs, and actions. Taken this way, it is easy to recognize a goal is just one step on our longer journey toward achieving our vision. When we achieve a goal, we are that much closer to making our vision a reality.

Returning to the ambitions we have discussed throughout this chapter, it is easy to see how vision can also play a vital role in obtaining achievements. For example, if you want to lose 10 pounds, your vision statement may be: "To become slim, fit, and healthy for life." If you want to buy a new car, a lofty vision statement might read: "To possess the latest in personal transportation technology." (Then again, a simpler version might be: "To enjoy the freedom and mobility transportation provides.") If you want to get married, your vision statement may be: "To face the future as part of a loving, supportive family," or "To commit myself to my spouse and children, building a household of love and support." Last, if you want to a new job or promotion, your vision statement might be: "To rise as far as possible in my chosen profession," or "To achieve financial independence while bringing maximum value to a business organization."

However you choose to write your vision statement, be bold. Be ambitious. It doesn't matter if you never quite achieve your vision. Or in the words of advertising genius Leo Burnett, "When you reach for the stars, you may not quite get them, but you won't come up with a handful of mud either."

Contemplation:

"Is my current situation aligned with the vision of who and what I want to be?"

Exercise: "The Superhero Analysis"

1. Make a list of your top 10 "superpowers." What things can you do particularly well? Sing? Dance? Problem solve? Persuade? Debate? Cook? Play videogames? Make this an intense brainstorming exercise.
2. Next to each superpower, list an action step that supports that power. Visualize putting your power into action. For example, imagine singing in front of a huge, enthusiastic crowd, delivering a TED Talk, or slaying your opponent in a political debate.
3. Assign each superpower to a goal you wish to achieve. Look for creative ways to put each of your abilities to practical use.

*****

Affirmation:

"My thoughts, feelings, and actions align with my vision of myself."

Engagement

Engagement is the act of taking a plan and putting it into action. It's about changing from *thinking* to *doing,* wading into the mud, getting your hands dirty, dealing with real-world consequences.

Startup companies often begin with a business plan. Once finalized, they must complete a list of actions before ever making their first sale. These can include raising capital, setting up an office, buying/leasing equipment, hiring/ training employees, developing marketing materials, and prospecting customers. Similarly, artists can spend years experimenting with different styles, techniques, and media, but only know they've succeeded when they put their work on display. And designers of computer apps and games often invest thousands of labor hours designing their programs, but then must beta test their products by having them used by real people in real-world situations to expose bugs that would never show up in the sheltered world of laboratory development.

Likewise, now that you've prepared yourself to pursue your goal, it's time to—in the words of the famous Nike ad campaign—*Just Do It.* If you want to lose 10 pounds, it's time to actually change the type of foods you eat and how much. If you want to buy a new car, it's time to start visiting dealerships or checking listings online. If you want to get married, it's time to start dating. Seriously. If you want to get a new job or promotion, it's time to start answering job postings, sending out your resume, or letting your manager know exactly the kind of position you really want.

For many people, this type of action is the most difficult step. More often than not, efforts of this type are met with frustration, rejection, and even humiliation. (Hey, if it was easy, everyone would be doing it, right?) That's why you have to be resolute. You have to be determined. This is why you have to reject fear and doubt, why you have to push forward, no matter what.

It's why you have to be BRAVE.

Contemplation:

Make a list of the steps, small and large, needed to create the best outcome you envision. What is the first act you need to take toward the first goal? When and how will you take it?

Exercise:

Create a roadmap to your goal. Take the first action on your list. Then the second. And so on.

Affirmation:

"As I take each step toward my goal, the next step appears."

Quote:

"Intentions are not visible. *Only actions are visible.*"

Now that we have explored how you can be BRAVE in your life; it may be helpful to reflect on some recent work I did with a client. The following is the story of an individual I helped push past fear to accomplish goals that once seemed beyond the realm of possibility.

Case Study: Shiv

Shiv is a 47-year-old Caucasian intersex male. Though Shiv was born with the reproductive organs of both genders, he identified as male early on. This greatly affected his feelings of self-confidence and self-worth. When he first came to me, Shiv reported suffering from debilitating fears of rejection. He told me that though he had dated members of the opposite sex, the experience had been understandably difficult. For a long time, he harbored fears his anatomy would handicap relationships for the rest of his life.

State of Mind

Shiv battled his lack of confidence and numerous insecurities. His fears would sometimes manifest as uncontrollable anger, exacerbating problems made worse by lack of strong coping skills.

Situation

At the time we began working together, Shiv was not in a relationship and he felt unsatisfied with his job. Although he looked to be the picture of masculine virility and identified as a male, he nonetheless saw himself as part of the transgender community (because it is not judgmental).

Status

In addition to desiring a romantic partner, Shiv wanted to change careers, but was unsure of how to go about doing so. Uncertain how he appeared to others, he often felt his male/female energies were out of alignment.

Becoming BRAVE

Beliefs >>> *Benevoliefs* (A Perfect Man):

Shiv believed his physical anomalies limited his professional and personal options. I encouraged him to adopt the *benevolief* that his male and female energies combined to give him superpowers to change his life, and that his unusual anatomy is, in fact, a gift.

Readiness (Now is Shiv's Time):

Using self-awareness exercises (involving a new conception of anatomical beauty, as well as the blending of male/female energies for personal power) we uncovered areas for Shiv to manage better:

Sleep:

A new bedtime routine incorporating music to aid with internal conversations.

Positive Energy:

10 minutes of mantras/affirmations per day.

Anxiety/Anger:

Daily journaling to relieve emotional overloads.

Education:

Recommendations of 30 minutes per week to learn more about depression and its physiological manifestations.

Alignment (Going Inward to Get Okay with the Outward):

Shiv turned his creative, spiritual interests into formal healing practices mirroring his values and identity. Opening up and sharing his techniques with others in transgender group sessions not only delivered a feeling of contentment, it also allowed Shiv to expand his confidence and feelings of self-worth.

Vision (Extending my Hands):

I asked Shiv to write a personal vision statement about who he is and who he wants to be. This statement was to incorporate his professional goals—to find greater purpose in his work—and to learn more about himself from new, healthier perspectives.

Engagement (Conquering Thyself):

Shiv worked diligently to learn new coping mechanisms to control his anger and other challenging emotions. He practiced mindful communication to prepare for future romantic relationships.

Outcomes

Shiv increased his personal power and self-confidence through the practice of using his energies toward spirituality and artistic expression. He became more mindful in life, aware of how his behavior and choices were affecting his relationships, his career progress, and his overall health.

What I Learned from This Client

My work with Shiv reminded me of the importance of balancing one's energies, not only masculine and feminine, but also introversion and extroversion, light and dark. I realized more fully how our society places binary constraints on people, even though they may not fit conventional molds, and how we cannot allow these labels to control other people's perceptions of who we really are.

Quote:

"Sometimes you have to plan a new attitude to experience a change."

For contemplation:

Do you feel you have a purpose? If so, what is it? If not, how does that make you feel?

Affirmation:

"My purpose is an imperative one that will make an impact on myself and others."

Exercise:

Discovering your purpose can be a major breakthrough. Do you know yours? If not, begin by asking people who are closest to you, "What do you believe my purpose is? How does my life impact yours?" Write down the responses, then combine them with your own thoughts to develop a clear, single statement about who you are and what you are here to accomplish. With this realization in mind, prepare, then *execute* an action plan that makes this purpose a reality.

Chapter 10
Let's Be Brave Together

One does not become BRAVE in a vacuum. Personal growth occurs as the result of multiple interactions with numerous individuals under varying conditions over long periods of time. Or as the father of modern physics, Sir Isaac Newton, taught us, for every action, there is an equal and opposite re-action.

Every book I have ever read, every seminar I have attended, every teacher who has mentored me, and every client I have served, has had an impact on who I am, what I believe, and my choices. At the same time, my journey has affected the people with whom I have interacted. So far, I have told you my story and some of my clients. But I also wanted to share with you the voices of those closest to me, to see how being BRAVE has influenced their lives.

Knowing in particular, how much Umesh has impacted chapter after chapter in this book, I only felt it fair to give him his due, to reflect on our relationship. But first, let's turn to my daughter for her perspective...

Sanam

My daughter, Sanam, was born on December 3, 2000. As of this writing, she is 18 years old and about to go off to college as a freshman. In the following conversation, she discusses her upbringing as the child of divorced parents and how the tenets of BRAVE have influenced her life.

What were the challenges you faced as the only child of a troubled marriage?

"I feel like I grew up faster than the other kids in my class. We were not a happy family. Every day, I woke up asking, 'Is today going to be normal, or is there going to be a fight?' I saw very little of my father when I was younger. He would go out and not return until late or, in some cases, the next morning. He also didn't attend many of my school or athletic events. When he was home, he was often hung over or disoriented from his medication's side effects. He and Mom would get into fights, usually about money. He would try to take the credit cards. She would hide them."

Who were your role models as a young child?

"I have to say my mom. The fact that she was able to take care of me, run the household, and still be married to my dad was quite a feat. I really appreciated that she was able to take me to events and play the role of both mom and dad when she needed to. In my eyes, she was really brave, and I appreciate her for that."

Do you look up to your father?

"My dad did a real 180 in his life. Defying a lot of people's expectations, he completely overcame his drinking addiction. He transformed himself, and in the process, truly accepted the role of being a father. He knows he screwed up and wants me to have a life completely opposite from the one he had. Nowadays, he never stops trying to make sure he's taking care of me, helping to guide me in ways he didn't in the past. He uses his truth to motivate me to lead a strong, clean life."

Do you blame either of them for the divorce?

"Not at all. As I have grown, I have learned firsthand that it takes two people to break up a marriage. My parents taught me not to blame others for my problems, but to accept responsibility for my actions. I'm glad to see that they're now able to cooperate and remain good friends."

What were the greatest lessons you learned from the challenges you experienced growing up?

"Probably the biggest lesson I learned is that going through a hard time doesn't give you license to just think about yourself or to stop helping others. That's something my mom models. Even though she had personal difficulties, they didn't stop her from becoming a life coach or teaching others through her experiences. I try not to blame people for my problems. Instead I try to help those going through things that are even worse. I also learned about independence and resilience—especially to avoid self-pity and not to let obstacles stand in the way of doing what I want or what I believe is right."

What advice, if any, would you give your parents today?

"I'd advise them to give back in their own way. To be there for those that need them. To be their authentic selves and live their truth."

Do you think your parents are living authentically now?

"Yes! It took them a long time to get there. Decades, actually. But they're now living the lives they were meant to live."

When it comes to living bravely, whom do you look to these days as a role model?

"I would say it's my dad because I already know all of the great things about my mom. But my dad really changed his whole life. What's brave about my dad is that many of the people who know us have seen his more embarrassing times. Yes, he's done stuff others looked down upon. But after he committed to change, he got right back into the role of a dad and has never failed to be there for me. Right alongside my mom."

Umesh

Umesh arguably had the greatest impact on my life. He was my first true love and my husband for more than a dozen years. And, of course, he remains the father of my one and only child. As the previous pages attest, Umesh's alcoholism and bipolar tendencies created strains that tested my character like no other. If diamonds are created by heat, pressure, and time, then Umesh provided the stresses that ultimately crystalized the beliefs I hold today. As I completed this book, Umesh, who still lives in the same city as I do, agreed to speak about our relationship, our history, and his interpretation of BRAVE.

Is there any one person you blame for your divorce?

"It was probably all my doing. Anita and I knew each other for a long time, and for a while we were comfortable with our lives. But as time went on, what we wanted from the marriage began to change. I know I became frustrated, and I started drinking. Later, I was diagnosed as bipolar. She probably expected things from me I could not give her. Eventually, we had to leave each other. Although, in a way, you could say I was really running away from myself."

But you still love each other?

"Yes. I still love her, and I believe she still loves me. You can't live together as long as we did without those strong feelings remaining."

Have you seen a change in Anita following your divorce?

"Anita has always been a very nice person. Always very loving. And very expressive. Maybe too expressive at times, trying to resolve issues on the spot. Life sometimes requires time and space."

In terms of this book, do you think Anita found bravery or has she always been that way?

"From my perspective, she has always been a strong, independent person. She came from a strict background in which her role in life was clearly defined. Even so, she never cared what other people thought about her. She was never afraid of being judged. She always knew what she wanted and what she was going to do. If she wanted something, she would just do it. For example, when we were young, she would drive from Mission Viejo all the way to the city of Bell, which is a good 45 minutes by freeway in clear traffic, just to see me for 10 minutes so we could spend some time together. I consider that brave."

In what ways might a *mindshift* helped save your marriage? Could a change of attitude or perspective have prevented the dissolution?

"Certainly, our attitudes toward marriage contributed to our problems. Anita always looked at the practical aspects. She was willing to adjust this, fine-tune that, try anything to see if it would work. That's why she liked couples' therapy. I looked at marriage more as an ideal. I had a vision for what a marriage was supposed to be, and rejected anything that challenged this vision. Maybe if I had been more practical—more pragmatic— things would have worked out differently."

What have you learned from Anita?

"I have learned to not be fearful. To be open to change. And, of course, most of all, to be brave."

Case Study: Gia

Both Umesh and Sanam experienced the trauma of a failed marriage, albeit from different perspectives. And like me, they found that being BRAVE gave them the ability to *mindshift* away from the pain of divorce and toward more positive, constructive sentiments. My final case study in this book, Gia, also was the victim of a failing marriage. At the time I met her, this Indian-American woman was 42 years old. Although she was still living with her husband, she believed there was no long-term hope for their union.

State of Mind

When she came to me, Gia reported feelings of loneliness and insecurity. She felt unloved, abandoned, and neglected by her husband.

Situation

Gia and her husband hadn't slept together in a year; she suspected he was cheating on her but had no solid evidence. When she did initiate sex, he rejected her.

Status

Gia had been actively seeking ways to improve her situation, but so far had found no answers. She decided she needed outside help.

Being BRAVE

Beliefs >>> *Benevoliefs* (You Can Be What You Want to Be):

Gia was impeded by the belief she was not desirable or worthy of her husband's attention. We changed this to the *benevolief* that she is a beautiful, sexy woman with many wonderful gifts to share.

Readiness (Change Comes from the Inside):

To prepare herself, Gia needed to understand that change had to come from within. She couldn't just expect her husband to change.

Alignment (Lock, Meet Key):

Gia would ready herself for intimate connections with her husband. Such intimacy was more significant than the bedroom, it included mental, emotional, spiritual and physical elements.

Vision (No One Can Give it to You; You Must Take It):

Gia's vision is to be a woman whose value is not determined by her husband. Instead, she wished to find validation within.

Engagement (Making it Happen):

Gia put her BRAVE plan to work by decluttering both her house and her mind, clearing away distractions.

She began exercising to lose weight, and actively sought opportunities to make herself feel feminine and desirable.

Outcomes

Since working together, Gia has found a new career role in the education field. This professional success has impacted her marriage positively. She and her husband now enjoy a more balanced relationship. Together, they are working to improve their intimacy through greater communication and understanding. She is taking better care of herself, watching her diet and maintaining a daily exercise regimen. She is also being mindful not to react fearfully fear whenever faced with an unexpected setback. Mindful communication has been instrumental in creating this *mindbreak* from defensive reactions to negative events.

What I Learned from this Client

My work with Gia reminded me that all the work is internal before it is external. Get right with yourself and you will be right with the rest of the world.

I was also reminded that relationships that create a dependency in either direction (or both) are not good. A positive, healthy relationship is a partnership between equals. Finally, I was reminded intimacy exists on many levels. Too often we equate it with physical contact, whereas intellectual and emotional connections can be just as powerful, perhaps even more so.

Quote:

"It's a choice if you want to cross that bridge; when I did the view was better."

For contemplation:

Describe one time you felt insecure in a relationship. What helped you (or would have helped you) feel more secure?

Affirmation:

"I am worthy of a loving and passionate relationship."

Exercise: Couples Connect Workout:

1. Address and confirm your communication styles. Are you one who likes to communicate face to face? By phone? Scheduling time away in a public place?
2. Create and validate your sacred language involving healthy communication, adoration, and respect. Address one another with any special names (e.g., "Honey," "Dear," "Darling," etc.)
3. Make time to thank your partner for the lessons they have provided you. Approach the other person with humility, focusing on their strengths.

Epilogue

I am not the first person to write about the mental and spiritual approach to self-improvement, nor, I am sure, will I be the last. There are many researchers, therapists, physicians, psychologists, and motivational experts who have written extensively on this topic. Many of these books have gone on to be best sellers. Their insights and wisdom have slowly found their way into our mainstream culture, changing how we think about ourselves and our approach to problems in our personal and professional lives. Great understanding and support can be found in many of these books, revelations that in combination with my own life and experiences, helped me create BRAVE.

Beyond drawing inspiration from this book, I strongly encourage you to read as many of the below authors as possible. True wisdom does not spring from a single source, but is an amalgam of hundreds, if not thousands, of inputs. Or to quote our friend, Sir Newton again: "If I have seen further, it is by standing on the shoulders of giants." In this spirit, I offer the following personal recommendations to further your growth and development:

***BLINK: The Power of Thinking Without Thinking (2005)* by Malcolm Gladwell**

In this slim (188 pages), eminently readable book, popular science author Malcolm Gladwell explores how people are wired to make snap judgments based on only fragmentary information. He calls his process "thin-slicing," and explores both the advantages and disadvantages to making split-second decisions.

From *The New York Times* 2005 review by critic David Brooks: "There is in all of our brains, Gladwell argues, a mighty backstage process, which works its will subconsciously. Through this process we have the capacity to sift huge amounts of information, blend data, isolate telling details and come to astonishingly rapid conclusions, even in the first two seconds of seeing something. *Blink* is a book about those first two seconds."

INSTINCT: The Power to Unleash Your Inborn Drive (2014) by T.D. Jakes

In this book, evangelist Bishop T.D. Jakes, pastor of The Potter's House, a non-denominational American megachurch, shows readers how to tap into their God-given intuition to achieve personal and professional success. Jakes believes that we all hold within us the power to succeed by simply following our natural inclinations and provides numerous examples of how this can—and has—been achieved.

From critic Saji Ijiyemi's 2014 book review on sajigroup.com: "You will gain a lot from reading *Instinct*. Not only will you be able to take inventory of what is inside of you, you will also learn how to cut to the core to discover what is in you. You will learn how to struggle through and survive life transitions, how to deal with predators in the jungle of business, political, religious life. Fact or faith? Data or drive? Gut or brain? T.D. Jakes showed how we can strike a balance between instinct vs. intellect, intuition vs. information, when to go vs. when to grow. Buried in the pages of this book is how to live by instinct, love by instinct, learn by instinct, and lead by instinct. If you know you have what it takes but need a guide on how to take what you have, you need to read *Instinct*."

GRIT: The Power of Passion and Perseverance (2016) by Angela Duckworth

Angela Duckworth is the founder/CEO of Character Lab, a nonprofit dedicated to the science of character development in children. In this book, she details how anyone striving to succeed can achieve their goals not via talent, training, or even luck, but through a special blend of passion and persistence she calls "grit."

From the 2016 *New York Times* review by Judith Shulevitz: "If this book were a Power Point presentation, as it surely has been, the best slide would be the two equations that offer a simple proof for why grit trumps talent: Talent × effort = skill. Skill × effort = achievement. In other words, 'Effort counts twice.'

"My grandfather, an immigrant, knew this. He would have called grit *Sitzfleisch*. (Malcolm Gladwell, in his best-selling *Outliers*, called it the '10,000-hour rule.') Moreover, you don't just need *Sitzfleisch*. You need focused *Sitzfleisch*. Thirteen-year-old Kerry Close logged more than 3,000 hours of practice to become the National Spelling Bee champion, but that wasn't the reason she won. Close's competitive edge came from her fearless approach to practicing. At her tender age, she had the guts to identify and fix her mistakes, over and over again."

COURAGE TO CHANGE: One Day at a Time in Al-Anon II (1992) by Al-Anon Family Group Head Inc.

"God, please grant me the courage to change ..." is the first line from the Alcoholics Anonymous serenity prayer. This 380-page book contains a page to read for each day of the year. It provides the comfort, hope, and affirmations we all need to get through the challenges of daily life.

UNLIMITED POWER (1986) by Anthony Robbins

I have written repeatedly about the enormous influence Tony Robbins has had on me, and this seminal book, written back in 1986, will help you understand why. In it, he argues that via a technique called "neurolinguistic programming," people can literally talk themselves into success. He shows how we can increase our emotional well-being, build our self-confidence, and achieve financial freedom by ignoring our limits, emphasizing our strengths, and having the confidence to take risks.

MY VOICE WILL GO ON WITH YOU: The Teaching Tales of Milton H. Erickson (1982) with Commentary by Sidney Rosen

Milton H. Erickson was a renowned hypnotherapist who pioneered the use of telling stories as part of his therapy. This book, edited by his colleague, Dr. Sidney Rosen, contains dozens of tales designed to help people overcome habitual limitations, reframe traumatic experiences, and discover their deepest values.

From the 2019 review on Uncommon Knowledge (www.uncommon-knowledge.co.uk): "During the course of therapy, Milton H. Erickson would frequently tell seemingly unrelated stories. Tales of previous clients, his family and other apparent trivia peppered his sessions, both in and out of hypnosis. This book is a collection of some of his most famous stories and case studies with a friend of his, Sydney Rosen, providing the context."

THE WISDOM OF INSECURITY (1958) by Alan W. Watts

Alan Watts was a British-American philosopher who helped translate and popularize Eastern philosophy and mysticism for Western audiences. He wrote more than 25 books and articles during his brief life and is probably best known for having introduced the ancient concept of "Zen" to American youth culture in the late 1950s.

From the Los Angeles Times: "Perhaps the foremost interpreter of Eastern disciplines for the contemporary

West, Alan Watts had the rare gift of 'writing beautifully the un-writable'. Watts begins with scholarship and intellect and proceeds with art and eloquence to the frontiers of the spirit. A fascinating entry into the deepest ways of knowing."

****

In no particular order, here are a few more helpful books to aid in your journey of self-mastery:
- *The Untethered Soul: The Journey Beyond Yourself* (2007) by Michael A. Singer
- *A New Earth: Awakening to Your Life's Purpose* (2005) by Eckhart Tolle
- *The Seat of the Soul* (1989) by Gary Zukav
- *Twelve Rules for Life: An Antidote to Chaos* (2018) by Jordan Peterson
- *The Alchemist* (1988) by Paulo Coelho
- *A Return to Love: Reflections on the Principles of 'A Course in Miracles'* (1992) by Marianne Williamson
- *The Four Agreements: A Practical Guide to Personal Freedom* (1997) by Don Miguel Ruiz
- *Tuesdays with Morrie* (1997) by Mitch Albom
- *Think and Grow Rich* (1937) by Napoleon Hill
- *The Last Lecture* (2008) by Randy Pausch and Jeffrey Zaslow
- *The Seven Spiritual Laws of Success: A Practical Guide to the Fulfillment of Your Dreams* (1994) by Deepak Chopra

A Fond Farewell

Ultimately, it's our challenges that shape us, helping us to define who we are as individuals. Or as Tony Robbins once said, "The only 'problem' we really have is we think we're not supposed to have problems. Problems are what make us grow. Problems are what sculpt our soul. Problems are what make us become more."

The preceding pages have been my attempt to describe the obstacles I faced. It's my deepest wish that by sharing them—by exploring what they taught me—they have offered you insight as to how to face your own. No one's life is easy, but that's okay. Dealing with adversity helps transform us from the inside out, forcing us (whether we like it or not!) to become the souls we are meant to be.

Before parting, I would like to thank you for reading this book. It's been the joy of my life to present you my story. I hope it helps you navigate your own. In parting, I wish to offer you one final blessing: Though your life may offer its share of unique challenges, I hope you rise to the occasion by being BRAVE. For we cannot control what comes at us, we can only choose how we respond.

~Sincerely,
Anita Kanti, 2019

Acknowledgement

This book would not have arrived at fruition if it had not been for the individuals who contributed their time, trust, and faith in my vision. We only grow through life experiences that we choose to be a part of, regardless of the outcome. I would not be the woman I am today without the ones that were strategically placed in my life, whether they were welcome or otherwise.

I sincerely thank my writing coach and partner, Michael Ashley, whose talents, understanding, and friendship throughout has been a gift. I also wish to express my gratitude to Umesh, my first love. I am lucky to have connected with him as well as our daughter, Sanam, whose support and courage I admire.

And thanks to my clients, whom I consider some of the bravest individuals I have ever met. Their stories demonstrate how we can accomplish tremendous and meaningful change through *mindshifting*. I value, honor, and appreciate their confidence in me.

I have been blessed with wonderful, supporting parents and sisters whose love I cannot live without.

We should appreciate the friends and colleagues who tell us the truth in joyous and difficult times, while encouraging us to be a better version of ourselves. It was Rachelle and Michael who said I should share my story and write a book, and for that I say, 'Thank you."

I wish you all an abundant life BEHAVING BRAVELY.

~Anita K

About the Authors

Anita K

Anita K has been featured on nationally syndicated radio shows, including *Out of Office, Hire Power,* and *Like a Real Boss.* She is the Life Coach Resident Expert for the podcast *Life at the Office* and co-producer of YouTube's *The MAK Show* offering insightful life strategies.

She sees a gap in our culture to strategically help individuals, families, and corporations alike, not just survive, but thrive. An onsite coach for multiple organizations, she also leads TG Rainbow, a transgender support group. She coaches her individual clients through life transitions, relationships, cultural identity management, career advancements, and develops unique solutions to achieve their personal goals.

A graduate of USC in marketing, Anita worked in the corporate sector for years. Building on this experience, she also now coaches professionals in the workplace. With an emphasis on supporting top global tech firms, she mentors execs and employees alike in techniques for leadership growth, individual talent development, career search strategies, and gender gap awareness.

Excitement, service, and passion infuse Anita K with a unique affinity for unlocking limitless solutions for life's many challenges. Her message is simple: only by peering within and doing the hard work to *mindshift* will we ever find true peace and fulfillment.

Michael Ashley

Michael Ashley is a best-selling author who has written books for thought leaders in numerous sectors. A regular contributor to *Forbes* and *Entrepreneur*, he has appeared on numerous radio shows and podcasts and has been featured in *Entertainment Weekly*, *The National Examiner*, The United Nations' *ITU News Magazine*, *Pelican Hill Magazine*, *The Orange County Register*, and the *Orange County Business Journal*.

Prior to founding his own creative content company, Ink Wordsmiths, he worked as a screenwriting consultant to Disney, a magazine columnist, a copywriter, blogger, and newspaper reporter.